HUMANE EDUCATION DEPARTMENT

Canines in the Classroom

Canines in the Classroom

Raising Humane Children through Interactions with Animals

Michelle A. Rivera

Foreword by Randall Lockwood, Ph.D.
Afterword by Michael Berkenblit, D.V.M.

2004
Lantern Books
One Union Square West, Suite 201
New York, NY 10003

© Michelle A. Rivera, 2004

All rights reserved. No part of this book may be reproduced, stored in a retrieval system or transmitted in any form or by any means, electronic, mechanical, photocopying, recording or otherwise, without the written permission of Lantern Books.

Printed in the United States of America

Library of Congress Cataloging-in-Publication Data

Rivera, Michelle A.
Canines in the classroom : raising humane children through interactions with animals / by Michelle A. Rivera ; foreword by Randall Lockwood ; afterword by Michael Berkenblit.
p. cm.
Includes bibliographical references.
ISBN 1-59056-053-1 (alk. paper)
1. Humane education. 2. Moral education. 3. Children and animals.
I. Title.
HV4712.R58 2003
370.11'4—dc22
2003022325

Acknowledgments

I WOULD LIKE TO THANK the following people for their contributions to this project:

My husband, John, for believing in me; Dr. Randy Lockwood, Dr. Mary Ann Jones, Dr. Mary Lou Randour and Peggy McKeal for their insight into psychology and emotions; educators Vanessa Reeves, "Coach" Wesley Holiday, Kay Heisler, John Harvill, Jady Hill, Greg Dulkowski and "Miss Kay" for allowing me into their classrooms week after week and sharing their amazing students and expertise with me; Dr. Mike Berkenblit and Dr. Lisa Degen for their friendship, love, support and, of course, their dogs, Woody and Katie; Village Animal Clinic and the Peggy Adams Animal Rescue League for enormous support and sponsorship; Judy Johns, Ann Gearhart, Kelley Ann Filson, The Association of Professional Humane Educators, Caroline Crane, Linda Jo Fields Horse, Penny Milkins and Abby, and all of the humane educators who answered the survey, sent photos or helped with the creative process; my dear friends Stephanie Linton and Karen Garcia for keeping me balanced during the long process of writing a book; Dianne Sauve and David Hitzig for their contributions on wildlife issues; Marge Sargent for all her research and hard work on the appendix; Lt. Sherry Schlueter, who is my cherished friend and mentor, Bernard Orestes Unti, Wayne Pacelle, Karen Davis, Susan Roghair, Dr. Steve Best and all my animal rights friends whose expertise on so many animal issues helped with this project; my (long-suffering) editor Sarah Gallogly, Detective Cassie Kovacs, who fills my world with wisdom and understanding (and my workspace with aromatherapy); and my sons, Jay and Toby Rivera, who share my concern for stray, hurting and lonely animals (especially meezers).

Canines in the Classroom
is dedicated to my
mother in law,
Marion Marcasiano Rivera,
who lovingly raised all her children to be humane,
compassionate
and filled with empathy.
Her legacy lives on in generations to come.

and to Woody and Katie Berkenblit
The quintessential Hospice Hounds

Finally, this book is in memory of Nathania Gartman, called home on July 3, 2003 after a courageous battle with breast cancer. She was a wonderful teacher and friend to the animals.

Table of Contents

This time . . .

I may have been a feline
I may have been a bird
or possibly reptilian
and couldn't
speak
a word

I may have suffered greatly
I may have felt so small
though I could have been a mammoth
Herculean,
strong
and tall

Whatever the injustice
that I suffered while so mute
I'll harbor deep inside my soul
yet wear it,
like a suit

for now I am loquacious
I have a voice to share!
this time I can't be quiet
'til all is just
and fair

I may not take this path again
a being with free speech
so I'll not waste this precious chance
to say
to pray
to teach

—Michelle A. Rivera

Foreword

For many people, including many teachers, the image of "humane education" is still one of the nice lady from the local animal shelter making a one-time visit to a classroom to talk about pet care and the importance of spaying and neutering. I hope that *Canines in the Classroom* will clearly show how that represents a very small, but still important, part of what contemporary humane education is all about. Michelle Rivera is a great example of the new breed of humane educators whose teaching efforts encompass responsible animal guardianship, environmental awareness, character development, community involvement, violence prevention, peer relations, social justice and more. Humane education today is not a "frill," something to add on to the classroom activities only if time and budgets permit. It deals with the fundamental issues of our duties and responsibilities to family, friends, communities and all living things. There are new challenges associated with this evolving concept of humane education, and traditional approaches, including the role of animals in the classroom, need to be openly examined. Michelle has combined her knowledge of the field, her interviews with many professionals, and her experiences in and out of the classroom to produce a valuable reflection on the state of the art.

It is fitting that Michelle begins this book with the wonderful story of her pet duck, Daffy Down Dilly, and the role her mother's patience, empathy and compassion played in shaping Michelle's future path and career choices. We sometimes overlook the role of parents as the first and often most influential humane educators in children's lives. The values they instill, or fail to instill, and the examples they set provide much of the raw material that future teachers and humane educators will have to work with.

Like Michelle, I was fortunate to have a mother who nurtured and shared my interest in animals. One of my earliest memories is sitting with her watching a spider building its web in a corner of our living room. "That's her house," she said. "We'll leave it be." This simple lesson in tolerance and seeing the world through the eyes of another was the kind of experience that can gently produce a significant shift in perspective that lays the groundwork for a compassionate lifestyle. It also demonstrated that such a world view has its costs. My grandmother thought this exercise was merely a disgusting lapse of housekeeping and tried to sweep away the webs, to our protestations. Later, my mother kept a 3-foot-by-10-foot swath of our suburban yard unmowed, just to see what would grow and live there. She termed the bunch of weeds our "ecology patch," long before the term "ecology" had entered into mainstream vocabulary. Once again, our less tolerant neighbors saw this as sloppy lawn care and not an independent study of the suburban ecosystem. It is easy to recall these influences as I write this, surrounded by a library of books about bugs, even though most of my work in animal behavior has focused on dogs and wolves.

I strongly believe that most, possibly all, children are innately interested in other living things and inclined to assume that other creatures, like other people, experience the world in similar ways. However, this capacity for empathy, like the ability to acquire language and other skills, must be nurtured and stimulated. Hopefully parents will begin the process and teachers and others will enrich those skills. Unfortunately, many children do not have the benefits of such experiences, and many teachers lack the resources, time or experience to fill the void. Michelle describes many of her encounters with children and adults who have been intentionally cruel to animals. Some simply lack the knowledge that might help them understand how other creatures live and think and feel. Others are reacting to abuse and injustices they have experienced, trying to gain power and control over others in a world where they feel they have been denied any influence. Many of the offenders I have encountered, like some of those described by Michelle, seem to be people who have had their empathy starved or beaten out of them as children. Sometimes the damage is irreparable, but often the vestiges remain. As Michelle and others have discovered, interactions with animals, particularly dogs, can help make connections to an earlier, undamaged self and help to teach the person that caring for others is empowering, despite the risks of pain such caring might bring.

Working with children or adults who are considered to be "at risk" or who have committed offenses against animals or people is a relatively new role for humane educators, but it is an extremely important addition to the traditional role in the classroom or community. I feel it is particularly important to reach out to those who might benefit most from exposure to lessons of compassion and concern from others, and from interactions with humane mentors. It is also important to provide such resources to kids at the other end of the spectrum, the young activists who can guide and lead their peers in caring for and about animals.

Michelle has also tackled an issue that is of particular interest to me, the use and misuse of animals in the classroom. My own experiences in this area began more than twenty years ago when I first accompanied the late John Harris and author Scott Barry to dozens of classrooms accompanied by "wolf ambassadors" to teach children about wolf behavior and conservation. Taking wolves into classrooms is probably one of the most challenging efforts in education, offering great opportunities and potentially great risks. These were special animals, usually rescued from irresponsible owners or acquired from wildlife rehabilitation facilities. They were not pets, and the presentations made every effort to make that point and to promote tolerance and appreciation at a time when wolves were still widely feared and reviled. We often included a well-trained dog in our presentations to demonstrate the many differences between a companion animal and its wild counterpart.

Our presentations were enthusiastically welcomed by kids and adults. We visited countless nursing homes, children's hospitals and classrooms. The excitement and enthusiasm of the audience was uplifting and almost addictive. But it became apparent that for most people it was a superficial entertainment experience. The only groups that seemed to get the real message were the classes that had been well prepared on animal issues throughout the year, whose teachers we had been visiting for several years and who integrated the visits into a much larger curriculum. For the others, we were a few cool people with neat wild pets!

Undoubtedly we changed many people's ideas about wolves and helped educate many others about their fascinating natural history. These efforts were not without enormous anxiety and emotional costs. It took all our strength and skill to prevent one endangered species (the wolf) from devouring another (a bald eagle) on the stage of Carnegie Hall as part of Paul Winter concert and environmental fund-raising event. The heaviest emotional toll came when two of the wolves were poisoned in their traveling van in New York City. A few years later a third wolf, Slick, was touring schools in upstate New York with John Harris. Slick was released from his chain and shot by a farmer, allegedly because he was attacking livestock. We were able to prove that the wolf had been stolen, killed and taken to the scene without ever harming anything. We knew that we had touched the kids in the community when dozens showed up at the subsequent trial wearing "Slick" buttons, but the legal victory did not erase our sadness.

When Scott Barry, myself and others stopped using wolves in our programs, many teachers and students seemed disappointed, but having a large Malamute as part of the team helped keep the doors open to presenting such programs. Eventually I made the personal decision to stop doing programs with live animals altogether, although I recognize that there are contexts in which appropriate, well-cared-for animals can provide valuable learning experiences. This book offers great insights into how to do this responsibly and humanely.

The final chapters in this book focus on another subject close to my heart, the need to build humane concerns into the broadest possible community responses to violence. My interest in this approach also started about twenty years ago, when much of my free time was spent on the road with wolves. My "professional" interests included work on how animals were treated in families with a history of child abuse or neglect. Our findings of a high degree of overlap between violence to animals and violence to other members of the family seem almost clichéd in 2003. However, they continue to provide professionals in social services and law enforcement with valuable tools for recognizing and responding to violent or antisocial behavior at an earlier stage than might otherwise be possible. Although this focus on community violence may seem to be a departure from conventional humane and environmental education, it seems very consistent to me. A generation ago one of the major concerns for naturalists and biologists was the devastating impact of pollutants and pesticides on animals and the environment, described most eloquently by Rachel Carson in *Silent Spring*. Today our concerns have shifted to what James Garbarino has called "socially toxic environments," plagued not by chemicals but by violent behavior that begets even more violence. Prior to the rise of ecological perspectives emphasizing the interconnectedness of animals and the environment, many of the components of living systems were viewed only in isolation from others. Likewise, communities have traditionally responded to violence by focusing on specific categories of victims—children, women, the elderly, animals—rather than looking at the interconnections and the roots of violence in ignorance, apathy and the destruction of empathy. Humane educators, like ecologists responding to environmental toxicity, can play a key role in helping people get the big picture of the ecology of violence in communities—violence that touches animals, children and others. This book provides practical suggestions for starting that process and for reaching out to children and others in ways that can help build a truly humane society.

Randall Lockwood, Ph.D.
Vice President/Research and Educational Outreach
The Humane Society of the United States
Washington, DC

May 2003

Preface

"Birds of a feather flock together."

—Anonymous

"Mrs. Lake, is that a duck?"

With these words, the Catholic priest who had come for tea exposed the deep, dark, secret we had kept so carefully. A duck lived in our garage. His name was Daffy Down Dilly.

As with millions of ducklings, this one was given to me when I was six as an Easter surprise. Remarkably, this tiny duckling shaped the way I was to regard animals for the rest of my life. Actually, there had been two ducklings that spring of '61, but one, regrettably, predictably, had succumbed to the overzealous lovings of a little girl who simply did not know that ducklings should not be hugged. How could I? It was years later, a half a lifetime really, before I understood that animals have their own way of showing love for on another, especially when they were not possessed of arms for embracing, but wings with which to fly.

My own Daffy Down Dilly grew into a fine adult duck who lived quite contentedly in our suburban backyard at 67 Daffodil Lane in Wantagh, Long Island, NY. When the neighbor behind us complained that Daffy had taken to flying over the fence so as to enjoy a swim in the luxury of their built-in pool, my parents scratched together a small sum of money and erected a 3 foot above-ground pool in which he could swim. They tried to meet his every need.

Not only that, my mother taught Daffy to dance. During rainstorms she would join him in the yard—trotting around with him, lifting her arms to the sky, even as Daffy lifted his snowy white, feathered limbs in wild flapping motions that amused me as I watched from indoors, nose pressed to the enormous picture window designed especially for the viewing of storms. "Dance, dance, dance" she would say, holding bits of bread just over his head and circling them around so that he would follow. Under the giant weeping willow tree, mom and Daffy would sing in the rain and dance the dance of a lone duck.

It was my mother's secret to harbor a duck. She kept his presence and existence hidden quite successfully from the church ladies, who would come visit and drink honey-laced tea. The jig was up one fateful day when Mom locked Daffy in the garage, dark and cool, with a small plastic toddler pool. This was his usual secret hiding place, of course, but this was not the usual tea-drinking ladies day.

The monsignor from St. Francis of Assisi where I went to school and we attended mass every Sunday, was coming for lunch. It was a long-awaited and eagerly anticipated visit. My mother positively radiated with the vitality of a young schoolgirl, as if awaiting a prom date! "Stay out of the way, Mike," she told me (using her pet name for me). "We have much to talk about, adult talk, so be a good girl and sit quietly reading your catechism. Please, oh please be good, Mike," she pleaded.

The setting was positively idyllic: the table set with fresh yellow daffodils the color of lemon chiffon, a crisp white Battenburg lace tablecloth, china teacups purchased just for the occasion, and fresh croissants from the bakery where we bought our hard-seeded rolls every Sunday after mass. And here, too, was a little girl in black tights and purple corduroy jumper, white starched blouse with Peter Pan collar and a velvet headband to hold back strawberry-blonde bangs that otherwise concealed the tiny widow's peak my mother insisted was a mark of great creativity, intelligence and yes, even psychic ability.

And herself, Kitty Lake, dressed in a bright turquoise blouse with three-quarter sleeves, starched white culottes and big, BIG white button earrings, wide plastic bracelet, and the huge cat's-eyes glasses that were the style back in 1962. She was fifty years old, quite "Rubenesque," and wore her hair in a champagne "bubble cut," the bouffant having just gone out of favor.

And finally, the esteemed priest, very tall and severe in his black clerical suit and white collar. He was an elderly man, but kind, and he greeted me with warm friendship. To my young mind, it was as if God himself had come to our home in Wantagh! If not God himself, then certainly, judging from the way my mother and all the nuns always acted around him at church and school, God's best friend and right hand man, his VP, his Lt. Colonel!

My mother practically exuded giddiness and excitement as she giggled nervously at his droll remarks and saw that he was comfortably seated. I slipped out into the garage to survey the car he had left in the driveway. A Lincoln, with back doors that opened in reverse! A big black Lincoln in our driveway! My friends would all think a movie star had come to visit! I tiptoed back into the house and my mother shot me a look that commanded, "Be good." Thus cautioned, I was dismissed.

I wandered into the living room and crouched down low so as to peek surreptitiously through the unique fireplace that had an opening in both the kitchen and the living room. Through the double black mesh screens, I could see these two adults, my mother and the parish priest, sitting at the table, my mother leaning forward, hanging on his every word.

I saw it first. I saw the door that led to the garage creak open just a tad. I hadn't closed it properly after my visit to the big black car! Tap tap, tap tap. The light tapping of a ducks bill forced the door open fully and in strolled Daffy Down Dilly. He waddled right up to the unsuspecting priest and took a healthy nip at his pant leg before continuing across the entire length of the kitchen floor. The priest put down his teacup and regarded the duck for a moment, my mother looking horrified and unable to react. "Mrs. Lake," he said quietly, "Is that a duck walking across your kitchen floor?"

My mother, recognizing the absurdity of it all, affected a thick Irish brogue and with a twinkle in her blue eyes responded, "Sure and I think 'tis, Faddah, 'tis a duck, 'tis himself, Daffy Down Dilly!"

I held my breath. My mother had just sassed the parish priest! Surely for this we would all go to purgatory unless we paid penance until the end of time! The priest regarded Mom for a moment, then broke into a wide grin and said, "I thought it might be." And the two of them laughed great gales of belly laughter that brought me scrambling to my feet and into the kitchen in a vain attempt to restore dignity and decorum to the moment. This sight, of course, brought only more waves of laughter until finally I succeeded in herding Daffy back to the garage.

My mother loved to tell that story.

It was very soon thereafter that my parents sat me down and with great solemnity told me that Daffy Down Dilly was very lonely because birds of a feather must flock together, and asked me how I would feel if there were no little girls for me to play with. They told me he needed to be with his own species and they knew of a farm where there were lots of ducks. I cried and cried and insisted that we visit this farm so I could see for myself how Daffy Down Dilly would live. So one bright, hot Saturday afternoon, we drove far, far out on the island until we came to a place with an enormous barn and a tiny lake and a small white building in the shape of a sitting duck, with a door where the chest would be. I was immediately on guard, picking up on the nervous glances and whispers of my parents. Something was wrong. We pulled up and stopped the car. A rough-looking man in overalls and a straw cowboy hat emerged from the barn and started towards the car. My dad told my mother and me to wait in the car, and jumped out. With only three long strides (he was 6'4") he met the man before he could come any closer.

After a moment, Dad nodded to the man and returned to the car. I held my breath but exhaled in relief when the turned the key and started the car. "This is not the place for our duck," he said. He turned to back out and caught my eye. Kindly, with great tenderness, he said, "We'll find another place, don't worry." And we went home.

At the time I did not know that ducks were considered food animals. My parents had certainly never served a duck for dinner, and I thought they were pets like dogs and cats, hamsters and gerbils, guinea pigs and rabbits. Much, much later, when I learned they were raised for food, the meaning of the looks my parents had exchanged that day became crystal clear.

Dad was a New York state trooper, and he knew something about state parks. He made a few phone calls and finally found a small state park on the North shore of Long Island, Caumsett State Park. Caumsett Park was a pretty place where people rented canoes and paddle boats, hunters were banned and roller skating and hiking among wildflowers were the main draw. This park had a beautiful lake that was home to several ducks and geese.

Again I cried the day we put Daffy Down Dilly in the car to take him to "duck camp."

"Can we visit him?" I asked hopefully.

"We won't know which one he is," Mom answered quietly.

"He wants to be with the other ducks now," Dad said. "He won't want us to hang around embarrassing him in front of all the other ducks."

"Noooo, I want to visit him!" I whined.

Mom spotted the Whalens' Drug Store in Cherrywood Center and told Dad to stop the car. She ran in and purchased a bottle of bright red nail polish. She showed it to me and explained that we would place a small red dot on Daffy Down Dilly's bill, not so big that the other ducks would laugh at him, of course, but enough that we would know him.

We released Daffy Down Dilly, but he didn't run to the other ducks. No, he stayed with us, a miserable group: A tall man, a tiny round woman, a little child and a duck. All standing close to the black Ford wagon with the wood on the sides.

We finally had to tear ourselves away, and Mom and I cried all the way home. But we went back a few days later and Daffy Down Dilly ran to us joyously, his red dot still very clear. Mom refreshed it to keep it bright. Eventually, our visits brought less enthusiasm from Daffy as he finally settled into duckdom and became, for the first time in his life at the age of eighteen months, a real duck.

This was my first lesson in humane education, and what a lesson it was! My parents never again made the mistake of buying an "Easter pet" (and as a mother, I never did, either).

I learned that animals need the comfort and security of kinship with their own species, and I also learned perhaps the greatest lesson of all. When we do a disservice to an animal, such as buying a duckling for a child on a whim, we must go to great lengths to right that wrong. We have domesticated animals and now, as their self-appointed stewards, we have a responsibility to them.

As humane educators, this is the message we bring to the schoolchildren of America.

• • •

Ducks and geese are routinely bought and sold by people wanting to use these animals as "ornamentals" in their ponds or pools. Luckily, there is not a big market for these animals, but a market does exist. There are all sorts of resources for people who wish to raise ducks and geese in an environment that is conducive to the welfare of these animals. And while animal-rights advocates and the people engaged in the business of raising "ornamental ducks and geese" are light years away from agreeing about the philosophy of owning animals for this purpose, there is one issue on which we can wholeheartedly agree: These animals are not suitable pets for little children. Children can easily crush tiny, fragile avian bones and kill a baby bird in a New York minute. Please don't purchase baby ducks, chicks or rabbits for little children.

Introduction

THERE IS A DUCK POND on the property of the local humane society. It's just there to the left as soon as you drive through the gate and down the long drive that leads to the shelter. It is a small pond, with a fan-fountain in the middle. It is inhabited by the likes of Daffy Down Dilly and his kind, as well as geese and mourning doves, pigeons and a lone guinea hen.

"The Domes" is what local residents have nicknamed the Animal Rescue League. It's a unique dome-shaped shelter, built that way to protect the animals from South Florida's terrifying and destructive hurricanes. There are three domes on the property. The first is a small white dome that has been divided into dwellings that provides housing for a staff veterinarian, a shelter manager and the night driver. Of course, their companion animals live there as well. No "no pets" policy in these apartments!

Then there are two larger domes, connected by a small vestibule. Inside, there is a veterinary hospital and animal shelter. The dogs and cats are housed separately, and there is a small boutique, humane education center and puppet theater. This is where I came to work after leaving the little veterinary clinic that I loved so much, so that I could become a humane educator working with schoolchildren and civic clubs. This would be a far cry from my experience with hospice patients, and I was looking forward to the challenges of working with children.

I never really left the place where I was always happiest, the Village Animal Clinic. The bonds that were built there have stayed strong, the people there remained in my heart and I have managed to involve many of their staff in working in the schools as well. My love for the "hospice hounds," Woody and Katie, and my admiration for them and their family, has only grown as I have seen them go from spiritual guides for the sick and dying to spirited guides for the young and light-hearted.[1]

It's not that Woody and Katie and I didn't like working in hospice, it's just that there is so much work to be done, and we, along with a few of our canine and feline friends, were called to teach compassion to children. "Character education," the experts call it, but Woody and Katie just want folks to know about taking care of animals.

It wasn't hard getting permission to take Woody and Katie to the classrooms. They are welcome wherever they go because they are so well behaved. The teachers call and set up the presentations, and I always ask if the dogs can come too. The teachers are provided a curriculum vitae of Woody and Katie's expertise, but this is never more than a formality. But then, it *should* be easy selling the idea that dogs are great teachers, because dogs have always been a part of our lives. In *The Pawprints of History*, Stanley Coren, the author of several books on dogs, urges us to realize that dogs have been serving humankind for fourteen thousand years![2] "The pawprints of many dogs are there," Coren writes, "but they are faint, and the winds of time erase them if they are not found and preserved." He recounts evidence that dogs helped save lives during the Lewis and Clark expedition and that Newfoundlands, St. Bernards and a plethora of "natural dogs" (also known as mixed breeds). I have saved countless lives in ways too numerous to chronicle. Witness the German shepherds who gave their lives during the Viet Nam war or the search and rescue dogs of September 11, and consider the variety of ways dogs are employed to help with functions from detecting seizures and heart attacks to "seeing" for the blind and "hearing" for the deaf. Dogs have long been a part of our lives, and it is only natural that we should turn to them for help in raising our children as well.

In some states, it is mandated that humane education be a part of the curriculum. In Palm Beach County, Florida, there is also a law that the county provide humane education, though the school board itself is not bound to that law. The idea of teaching children about responsible animal care and laws to protect animals was irresistible for me, and so I was easily recruited to come to the Animal Rescue League as director of the education department, as long as Woody, Katie and I came as a package deal. The Animal Rescue League was delighted to have us all join them. But you don't need to be working at a shelter to teach children about animals. You can do this on your own very well—and this book will show you how. *Canines in the Classroom* will help you find your way through the school system, give you the courage to reach for an obtainable goal and start us on our way toward a more humane, compassionate society. If the students that we reach through the ideas presented in this book grow up with respect for animals and the environment, compassion for all living beings and an eye toward a more sustainable future, then we will have accomplished what we have set out to do.

I wrote this book because there are fewer than one hundred professional, salaried humane educators in the United States, and this number is far too small. As one of those fortunate individuals, I hear from teachers and youth group leaders all the time about how important the work we do together is for the planet, the children and the animals. Every humane educator has a waiting list of teachers for whom there is just not enough hours in the day. We cannot get to them all.

That is why we need parents, teachers and others in the community to carry the torch for humane education. We need more humane educators out in the world, spreading the message of respect for all living things. For what we do to the tiniest of creatures, we do to ourselves. We truly are all connected in this web of life.

For those of you who share our vision for a more compassionate society, this book is a recipe for getting there. It is a blueprint for a society where everyone is treated with respect without regard to species.

In chapter one we learn about the concept and the history of humane education. We learn to light our tapers from the flame of knowledge that has been burning for centuries. In chapter two we see why teaching children to respect animals is such a natural thing to do.

Chapter three contains step-by-step instructions for getting a humane education program started in your own community and offers a few ideas on lesson planning. Chapters four and five deal with your animal partners who will be taking this journey with you. Why do we bring gentle dogs to classrooms across America? Whom does it benefit? Whom does it offend, and why? And chapter six discusses the related issue of classroom pets.

Chapter seven offers ideas on lesson planning, and chapter eight focuses on the therapeutic value that animals have to offer us as healers and tutors. Chapter nine presents some classroom teachers' perspectives on the benefits of humane education.

Chapter ten is devoted to lessons on a very important topic that is justifiably one of the most popular among humane educators: spaying, neutering, and the tragedy of overpopulation.

Chapters eleven and twelve address the darker side of humane education. This is where we take on the tough issues such as dog fighting and domestic violence. We hear from psychologists and scholars about the link between animal cruelty and violence to humans and what we can do right now to put a stop to violent behavior in our community. Chapter thirteen shares insights from clinical psychologists who have much to offer us in the theories of why violent children behave as they do and how best to teach them kindness and empathy.

Chapters fourteen through sixteen introduce us to others who are working in classrooms and communities to facilitate the bond between animals and humans, and offer suggestions on how to reach out to those who have not yet heard the good news about the need for animals in our lives.

Finally, chapter seventeen walks a while with those who are right there in the village that is taking the time to raise a child—the humane educators, classroom teachers and others who are blazing this trail for the rest of us.

Jane Goodall, the noted chimpanzee expert and internationally known anthropologist, in her foreword for *Strolling with our Kin* by Marc Bekoff, shares the story of her nephew, who, once he learned where fish came from and how they were killed for his dinner, refused to eat the fish. Clearly, nobody told him not to eat the fish. But once he learned on his own about fish, he made his decision. "When children have access to good information that enables them to have a good understanding of these issues, their logic is impeccable," writes Jane. "There is a new need for information that will encourage young people to understand the natural world and their relationship to it. A new need to reach children in school about the way their societies treat animals. And a new need to provide our youth with opportunities that foster respect for all life and an empathy with the animal beings with whom we, human beings, share the planet. . . . .We must encourage our children, empower them to help us save the world that will, so soon, be theirs."

Read, then go forth and teach. Let others light their candle from your flame.

Michelle Rivera
Jupiter, Florida
October 28, 2002

1

What is Humane Education?

"The purpose of life is a life of purpose."

—David Byrne

- A mother calls a local wildlife rehabilitator to report a baby squirrel that has fallen from his nest. She carefully follows the instructions given her on the phone. She does this in the presence of her nine-year-old son.
- A humane educator shows the video "The Power of Compassion"[3] to a group of high school students and helps them realize the power they have to stop the euthanasia of unwanted animals.

- A protester stands outside a pet store in the hot summer sun holding posters and passing out fliers illustrating "life" at puppy mills.
- A teacher encourages her students to follow the events in the newspaper as they relate to animals, then leads a classroom discussion about ethical considerations and issues surrounding animals.
- An activist persuades her local public television station to air *The Witness*.[4]

A member of a vegetarian club raises money to rent a booth at a county fair and hands out free samples, recipes and the booklet "Why Vegan?"[5]

These are all shining examples of what humane education is all about. Any time we take the time to fill another's cup from our own pitcher of knowledge, we are teaching. Teaching is the highest of all callings. If you doubt this, remember the story of the little boy who told his father he wanted to be a teacher. "But son," said his dad, "Don't you want to be something more important, a like a doctor or a lawyer?" "Who do you think taught *them*?" asked the boy!

Teaching does not have to involve a four-year degree and an overcrowded classroom. One can find opportunities to teach at every turn. World Animal Net describes humane education as "a process that encourages an understanding of the need for compassion and respect for people, animals and the environment and recognizes the interdependence of all living things." Rosemary Lyons, the humane educator for the Animal Control Division of Pasco County, Florida, said it best: "Humane education encompasses all of the issues that affect society in general. It touches on issues and asks questions that are not raised in any other area of learning. It helps children to formulate a personal code of ethics by combining the information with other types of learning."

According to the American Psychological Association, there are lots of issues that directly affect society "in general." Their studies show that the average child will witness at least eight thousand murders on television—in addition to more than one hundred thousand other assorted acts of violence—by the time he or she leaves elementary school. A 1995 study by the University of Pennsylvania Annenberg School for Communication found that in Saturday morning cartoons, cruel images of animals outnumbered positive ones by twelve to one.[6]

These astonishing and sobering facts leave little doubt that parents, teachers and others involved in influencing and shaping children's characters have much to do to neutralize the harmful images with which they are bombarded day after day. So what can we, as parents and teachers, concerned members and leaders of our community, do to help children form a more compassionate vision for their lives? We can introduce them to the wonders of animal life—dogs, snakes, cats, rabbits, horses and much more. And we can do this through a humane education program.

Humane education seeks to sensitize children to the varied attitudes and philosophies human beings demonstrate toward the animals with whom we share our world. Through a variety of fun and interactive lessons, we are able to gently guide students through the moral dilemmas brought to bear by exposure to a variety of belief systems and philosophies about our stewardship of the earth and the animals. The lessons taught within a humane education program have specific objectives and goals. If taught correctly, they should present the students with avenues for critical thinking and help them not only to understand that they should feel compassion for the creatures with whom we share our world, but also to recognize how they can put that compassion into action.

The nuns in the Catholic school where I was educated did not invite humane educators into the classrooms back in the '60s and '70s. I don't remember the public schools having any kind of humane education initiative, either. And I certainly don't remember my own children, now in their twenties, coming home with stories of a "dog lady" coming to visit their classrooms. Still, the concept of humane education is not new. In 1889 the American Humane Education Society (AHES, the educational affiliate of the Massachusetts Society for the Prevention of Cruelty to Animals) created and distributed humane education materials and implemented programs for schoolchildren. This was twenty-six years before the American Humane Association kicked off its first "Be Kind to Animals Week" in 1915, launching a poster contest for schoolchildren nationwide. In 1918, Edith and Milton Latham began the Latham Foundation for the Promotion of Humane Education. The Latham family became vegetarian in the year 1860, a bold move in the years devoid of Boca Burgers and textured vegetable proteins! And in 1928 Edith Latham promoted another poster contest within the public schools aimed at encouraging kindness toward animals.

Bernard Orestes Unti, a teacher in the history department at the American University, wrote about humane education in his dissertation "The Quality of Mercy: Organized Animal Protection in the United States 1866-1930."[7] The first discussions of compulsory humane education, Unti says, occurred in Massachusetts in the 1880s. Six years later, a humane instruction mandate was passed, and in the early 1900s a national campaign for mandatory humane education began to take shape and grow. In 1905, William O. Stillman of the American Humane Association and Stella H. Preston formed the New York Humane Education Committee to move forward a state-sponsored requirement that humane education be taught in the public schools. Later that year, Oklahoma and Pennsylvania passed laws requiring humane instruction as part of the "moral education" of future citizens, and mandated that half an hour each week be devoted to teaching "kindness to and humane treatment and protection of dumb animals and birds; their lives, habits and usefulness, and the important part they are intended to fulfill in the economy of nature."

It is not surprising that humane societies in the late 1800s and early 1900s were espousing the idea of kindness and compassion toward animals. What is exciting is that there was talk of humane education by the well-known and highly respected Parent-Teacher Association (PTA), a group having nothing whatsoever to do with animal welfare. The PTA embraced the idea of humane education in 1924. During that year, Mrs. Jeannie R. Nichols, the Chairperson of the National PTA Humane Education Committee, wrote about humane education in the pamphlet "Suggestions for Developing Humane Education Programs in Pre-school Circles and Parent-Teacher Associations."[8] Her words, written nearly a century ago, still ring true today: *"Children trained to extend justice, kindness and mercy to animals become more just, kind and considerate in their intercourse with each other. Character training along these lines in youth will result in men and women of broader sympathies, more humane, more law-abiding—in every respect more valuable citizens."*

In 1986, Dr. Randall Lockwood and the Humane Society of the United States (HSUS) working with the Federal

Bureau of Investigation (FBI), published "The Tangled Web of Abuse," a cooperative study that set out to prove the theory that there is a definite link between animal cruelty and human violence. The fact that many of the serial killers in history had admitted to committing acts of animal cruelty as children raised suspicions that children who perpetrate acts of animal cruelty and get away with them will grow up to be violent abusers who have little regard for human life. (More information on the link between animal cruelty and human violence, and the HSUS initiative and others like it, can be found in chapter eleven.)

If this is true, it elucidates the statement that "children trained to extend . . . mercy to animals" will become better citizens. Children who learn that animals have feelings and needs similar to ours will become more law-abiding, kinder and more humane to people and animals alike. What more can we ask for? What better characteristics are needed in our citizenry?

Ms. Nichols had still more to say; "Kindness is the one tongue that all human kind can understand that all creatures may be made to feel. It is the language that holds the balance of power in settling difficulties between individuals and nations, for, above all, a heart made kind means a mind above crime."

It is no surprise, then, that in some states there are mandates that humane education be a part of the curriculum. Some of the states that currently have humane education listed in their state statutes are California, Illinois, Maine, Massachusetts, New Jersey, New York, Washington, Wisconsin, Florida, Louisiana, North Dakota, and Pennsylvania. Some of the states have language that is clear and unequivocal.

In California, for example, the statute reads, in part,

(233.5. a) Each teacher shall endeavor to impress upon the minds of the pupils the principles of morality, truth, justice, patriotism, and a true comprehension of the rights, duties, and dignity of American citizenship, and the meaning of equality and human dignity, including the promotion of harmonious relations, kindness toward domestic pets and the humane treatment of living creatures, to teach them to avoid idleness, profanity, and falsehood, and to instruct them in manners and morals and the principles of a free government.

In Illinois, the statute calls for the "protection of wildlife and humane care of domestic animals," and in New York, the mandate is even more defined:

S 809. Instruction in the humane treatment of animals.

1. The officer, board or commission authorized or required to prescribe courses of instruction shall cause instruction to be given in every elementary school under state control or supported wholly or partly by public money of the state, in the humane treatment and protection of animals and the importance of the part they play in the economy of nature as well as the necessity of controlling the proliferation of animals which are subsequently abandoned and caused to suffer extreme cruelty.

Oregon calls for instruction in "humane treatment of animals," and in Washington State, instructors are to incorporate lessons in "the worth of kindness to all living creatures and the land." Louisiana has ordered that

The state board of education may take such steps as it may

> think necessary and wise to provide for the teaching of kindness to dumb animals in the public schools, it being understood that the state superintendent of education, by the direction of the board, will issue such suggestions and furnish such information to the superintendents and teachers as the board may deem appropriate and necessary
>
> .

In Florida the state statutes call for instruction on "kindness to animals." (Like many other states, Florida also mandates the humane treatment of animals that may be living in classrooms, prohibits using live animals for dissection, and addresses other animal issues not directly related to humane education.) However, individual county ordinances may make up for a lack of clear language in state laws. For example, Florida's Palm Beach County ordinance states,

> It is hereby considered to be a valid public purpose to educate the population of the county concerning the law and the proper care and respect for animals. In accordance with this duty, the Division shall make adequate provision for conducting appropriate educational programs.

Wayne Pacelle, Senior Vice President of HSUS's Communications and Government Affairs, comments, "The statutes came about because the humane movement was touting humane sensibilities as a primer for good citizenship. The thinking was that if you were taught to be humane in all your dealings, you would be a good citizen and you would be good to other people. I think it is great, it says something very important that we have these statutes on the books.'

Wayne continues, "It is important to raise kids with humane values because it is an investment in our future.

Young people will be around for another sixty to seventy years, and if you instill those values in a young person he or she will carry them throughout his or her life. The children of today are tomorrow's leaders. We know that kids have a natural affinity and inclination towards animals. They have not yet learned to commodify them; that comes later in life when people are taught to use animals. Young children, especially, have a natural bond with animals, and the goal is to nurture that compassionate instinct. Once you instill the values to go along with their compassionate instincts, you have laid the foundation for good citizenship."

Of course, whether or not a parent has ever heard of humane education, these foundations can be laid at home. But too often they are not. Dr. Mary Lou Randour writes in *Animal Grace*: "What was at first the parents' view of the child becomes the child's view of self. And then, feeling self-confident, he succeeds, which builds confidence—and confidence builds more confidence. As a child goes out into the world and meets others, he assumes that others will view him as his parents do—as a competent and reliable person. All of these experiences reinforce and deepen the child's sense of confidence. Of course, not all children have parents who are able to convey this sense to a child. Fortunately, it is not just our earliest relationships that form us, although they certainly are crucial. Relationships continue to form us throughout our lives. Teachers, peers, friends, and partners can all play substantial roles in our development."[9]

On the first reading, it may not appear that Dr. Randour's words have much bearing on humane education specifically. But she raises an important point for humane educators. If children are taught to be kind and compassionate, but lack self-esteem and a sense of individuality, can they still be expected to grow up to treat other humans and animals with respect? It is important that educators foster and encourage a strong sense of self-worth in children so that they won't feel a need to hurt other children or animals to build up their self-esteem. If we expect future generations to be more moral and just, our education of them must take a more holistic approach. Not only must we teach them to be kind to animals, other people and the environment, but we must also teach them to be kind to themselves. Today's generation, like the generations before them, face tumultuous times and difficult decisions. They are subjected to disillusionment, cynicism, pessimism and uncertainty every day. Their decisions can determine their status in their social circles as well as shape their futures. As children mature, they are forming opinions, attitudes and feelings. They are constantly measuring their positions against those of their peers. Most importantly, they want to fit in. Teaching children to have healthy self-esteem is one of the most important things we can do for the animals and our environment. After all, children who are diligently working to secure a future for themselves, to achieve a goal, children with ambition and insight, are not torturing animals and lighting fires. They are far too busy for that. They have nothing to prove. But what about those who do have something to prove? What about kids whose home life is so dysfunctional that they spend most of their days proving to themselves and those around them that they have worth?

Peggy McKeal is a licensed psychotherapist, a licensed mental health counselor and a national certified counselor in private practice in South Florida. She has extensive knowledge and experience of issues surrounding children. "I think it is fairly global to say that the kids who are fighting pit bulls are not the honor students," Peggy says. "You are going to find some children from very diverse backgrounds who really are very, very bright. I suspect that we can look at it culturally. The kids who are fighting pit bulls come from a different culture than most of the honor students whom we think of as white middle-class or upper-class kids. So pit bull fighting is done for ego strength and money. . . . they learn it from the adults who are fighting pit bulls. They grow up learning . . . that that is what makes them the tough guys on the block. Isn't it better to try to teach kids through compassion or raising their own self-esteem so they don't need that external sign (i.e., a pit bull) of their power?"

Peggy believes that the teaching of self-esteem is the most important thing and is the job of "society, the parents, the grandparents, the village and the school." It is not, she emphasizes, a one-hour course! But when these fail, can humane educators, who frequently may only have an hour or so with a select group of students, be expected to teach self-esteem?

Peggy approaches the task this way: "A long time ago I asked myself, 'What good am I doing?' I saw all these children with many serious problems and I thought 'I only see them for *x* amount of time . . . what *good* am I really doing?' And I had to really think about that, and I decided that if I can love them for the little time I have them, be it one hour or eight hours, if I can give them *from myself* a safe place to come back to, either in their own mind and heart or sometime later down the road, they can say to themselves, *I remember that lady, and this is how she felt, this is how she talked, this is how she listened; therefore there must be other people I can go to that I can get that same feeling from.* If I can give them that, that is an important thing. Even if it is only one kid that gets it, that's a hugely important thing. So humane educators, if they can go into the classrooms or go in the neighborhood and teach something different for one hour to one kid who then goes out later and spreads that message, it is very significant.

"Do I think that human educators can go into the schools and rectify all the huge problems of society? No, we would be foolhardy to think that. But can we help one kid, help one animal? Probably. And maybe that is enough, because that will spread exponentially. It will go from that child teaching another child or that child being an advocate. Where does advocacy come from? Something goes 'click' and an advocate is born. If the voice of the humane educator is quieted, the one child that may have heard you and become an advocate won't hear you."

Ann Gearhart, Humane Educator of the Year Award recipient for 2002,[10] told the following Cherokee folk tale to a group of humane educators gathered for a conference in Lafayette, Indiana.

> An old Cherokee is teaching a grandchild about life. He said, "A struggle is going on inside of me. It is a terrible struggle, and it is between two wolves. One is evil, anger, envy, sorrow, regret, greed, arrogance, self-pity, guilt, resentment, inferiority, lies, false pride, superiority and ego. The other is good, joy, peace, love, hope, serenity, humility, kindness, benevolence, empathy, generosity, truth, compassion and faith. This same struggle is going on inside you, and inside every other person too." The grandchild thought about this for a minute and then asked, "Which wolf will win?" The old Cherokee simply replied: "The one you feed."

Ann ended her story by encouraging those assembled to

continue to look for new ways to feed our communities what they need in the form of humane education. I hope humane educators, whether seasoned teachers or just starting out, will use this book as a tool to do just that.

2

A Natural Fit

"Teaching a child not to step on a caterpillar is as valuable to the child as it is to the caterpillar."

—Bradley Miller

I remember the first time I learned where hamburger came from. I was about six years old when I sat down to dinner one night and, surveying the contents of my plate, I realized that I knew the origin of an ear of corn, a potato and even the bread that the hamburger was sitting on. But looking at the brown slab of meat, I became puzzled. "Where did *that* come from?" I asked my parents. When I learned the truth, I looked at my mother in horror and disgust. I thought we liked animals! I was mortified to learn that the animals my parents had taught me to respect were being slaughtered for our food. My parents tried to console me by telling me, "That's just the way it is," and "We have to eat meat to survive; we have no other choice." Many years later, while watching an episode of *The Simpsons*, I watched a similar scene unfold in colorful animation as Lisa, having been to a petting farm and made friends with a tiny lamb, contemplates the lamb chops on her dinner plate. As she makes the connection between the food on her plate and the living animal, she imagines the lamb's beseeching voice: "But Lisa, I thought you loved me!"

Psychotherapist Peggy McKeal explains, "Children get so many double messages in their life that I suspect they grow up trying to justify things that they have an innate feeling of wrongness about." Like a person asleep or on autopilot, I continued to eat meat until I was well into my twenties, when I finally came to the conclusion that I no longer had to do what others did; I could follow my own conscience. Soon after I made the conscious decision not to eat meat, I saw a most disturbing photo in the newspaper. It did not depict a case of animal cruelty; rather, it showed a powerful example of the animal–human bond. A beautiful young pig named Tinkerbell pressed her sweet face against the bars of her cage and lovingly regarded the object of her affection, a ten-year-old boy. The boy sat cross-legged on the floor facing Tinkerbell, gazing into her eyes with a sad, defeated expression. He looked like he had just lost his best friend, or was about to.

The caption on the photo revealed this sobering story: The child had raised Tinkerbell from a piglet. He had carefully recorded everything she ate and documented her weight gain from week to week. Now, he had brought her to the fair to be sold at auction. He was saying goodbye, as thousands of 4-H kids had done before him.

As humane educators, we spend our days teaching our communities about the animal–human bond, the covenant we made with animals when we domesticated them—and how we have broken that covenant by mistreating animals, exploiting them and euthanizing them when their presence has become an inconvenience. We present educational videos of puppy mills, dog fighting and domestic violence involving animals in an effort to raise awareness of the sad fact that our society has become increasingly tolerant of animal abuse. We work constantly to demonstrate that empathy and compassion for animals fosters more compassionate citizens and a more compassionate society. But how do we compete with the message that it is appropriate to take an animal, nurture her and love her, see to her every need, bond with her and teach her to recognize your voice—and then, at the height of your friendship and unity, deliver her into the hands of slaughter and move on without a tear?

What are we teaching our children when we allow them to be responsible for a life and then take away that life in the name of capitalism and exploitation? Is there a mixed message here? On the one hand we teach children about love and respect, and on the other we tell them to invalidate those feelings when the fair comes to town. As adults and educators we encourage children to express their feelings, to rely on their own instinct and do what they think is right, not what others tell them to do. But those who raise pets for slaughter instruct them to deny those feelings, because it is right to slaughter their friends no matter what they feel about it. They tell children to be "strong," because "this is the way things are." *This* is why Tinkerbell was raised; *this* is the end result of all the shared love and affection, the dedication and responsibility. Ignore the fact that she feels pain, they say; ignore the emotional attachment and bond that the two of you have cultivated. In short, they say, ignore your feelings—we certainly do.

Dr. MaryLou Randour writes in *Animal Grace*, "Animals are significant, living beings in children's lives. Children do not experience them as abstractions or symbols. Adults may relegate animals to the periphery of their attention—but not children. What we sometimes call 'innocence' in children is actually unspoiled wisdom. Children are untainted by cultural prejudices created by the fear of otherness. They are free of social protocol that dismisses or demeans the position of animals in our lives. To children, animals are not lower—they are fellow beings of equal standing, worthy of the same treatment as a fellow human." But while we may begin our lives with this "untainted" relationship to animals, we rarely manage to maintain it. Before we understand what is happening—at the dinner table, at 4-H, or even at school—we are socialized to take a very different attitude toward animals.

For example, proponents of 4-H argue that the children understand from the beginning that the animals are being raised for food and that this fact makes it acceptable. Or they argue that children should know that the ham sandwich they consumed at lunch was once a pig like Tinkerbell. I understand that rationale; I just don't believe we have to take a life to make the point. Anyone who has ever seen the movie *Babe* understands the link between the living animal and the slab of bacon. And the fact that an animal is "raised for food" is of little consolation to the animal herself, who must suffer the pain of being torn from the child she has come to love and trust.

Kelley Filson is a humane educator for the San Francisco Society for the Prevention of Cruelty to Animals. At about the age of ten, she became a member of the 4-H club in her little town in upstate New Hampshire. To this day, she has not been able to forgive herself for the pain and suffering she inflicted on the animals she named and loved and nurtured and then betrayed. With tears in her eyes she recounted her feelings during that sad time in her life.

"I grew up in rural New Hampshire in a small town called Dunbarton. There were only eleven people in my first grade class, it was that rural. There was a wonderful old man who lived across the street who raised pumpkins and sold honey and cider and was a dairy farmer. Our family had geese, pigs, goats, cows, chickens. We did not have very much land. When I was about ten or eleven my brother and I decided to join 4-H. When you start 4-H the first thing you do is pick out an animal. We decided on sheep, and I think it was because my parents liked lamb meat. So we got two baby lambs.

"Lambs are usually born in February and you get them in the spring when they are weaned from their mothers. We had to do it quickly before the Greeks came because they would buy them up for the big Greek Easter celebration." (I thought of the gruesome scene in My Big Fat Greek Wedding where the skinned lamb is brought to the door and then cooked on the front yard on a spit.) Kelley continued, "So we drove to the farm and they put these baby lambs in blue bags with just their heads sticking out. Now the first thing you have to do is put a green rubber ring that is about the size of a Cheerio on their tail to remove the tail. They don't bother to do that if they are just getting slaughtered, but if you are going to be showing the lamb you need to remove the tail. They told us that tails can get infected and so they have to be docked. Now I think about wild sheep and how this is not required for them, of course. The green rubber ring is tiny, and it cuts off the circulation and eventually the tail falls off. Now I realize that that was painful for him, but at the time I was taught that it did not matter; it was what was needed to be done. I must admit there were other things that we did to the animals that I know caused them great pain. The green ring that we placed on the tail was also placed on the scrotum so that the testicles fall off. My lamb's name was Blue. I was in seventh grade. I had Daisy before that. These were just innocent little lambs. It seems so violent and senseless to put those animals through all that pain and misery."

It was a cold, snowy night and we were sitting together in a Holiday Inn in Lafayette, Indiana. Kelley, a pretty young woman with dark blonde curly hair and bright eyes, curled her long legs up under her body and took a moment to gather herself. Remembering the events of little more than a decade before had brought tears to her eyes and her voice trembled as she finished her story.

"The next thing you have to do is either tag or tattoo them. Some people tag their ear and the tag goes into a hole made in the ear that is about the size of a dime. But usually if the animal is to be shown you don't want a big hole in their ear so you tattoo them instead. A device that is similar to a hair crimper is used. It has holes in it where four to six numbers are placed like the old style print block settings. And you poke their ears really hard and then ink is rubbed in. So you puncture them, all these little holes, and then rub the ink in. That was very bloody and I know that it hurt them. The lamb ear is only a little thicker than a dog ear. . . . I think at that point in my life I had kind of been taught that this is what you do. My initial reaction, as for most kids, was: 'This is wrong—I don't want to hurt them, I don't want to see them die!' But we are taught that this is the role of the animal, that it's normal!

"They made us train our animals to work on a halter. They did not teach us humane methods for training, either. You drag the animal until they basically just give up and walk along with you. Nobody thought of bringing grain to kind of coax them along or put the halter on gently. Like now when I think about how I socialize my dog to his harness—if I had done that with sheep I would have been much happier. They would have been much happier! I felt horrible, but this is what the whole mentality is: you basically beat the animal into submission."

I wondered if this was what had brought Kelley to her role as a humane educator. Was she trying to stop other kids from living with regret?

"I am a humane educator now because I feel I need to make up for what I did to those animals," she agreed. "This is the conclusion that I have come to—it is as close as I can get to religion. When I die I want a clean conscience. For me that means, once I learn something new, if it has an effect on my life, if I know that I am doing something against my better judgment, then I really need to change my behavior. You hear things sometimes but don't really learn them. When I really learned the suffering that was caused by me I felt that in order to have a clean conscience I could no longer eat meat. When I finally grasped the [suffering caused by] consuming dairy products, I stopped consuming them, too.

"It's a growing, changing thing. At the time those animals in 4-H were killed for me I think I knew but didn't really grasp it. I wasn't fully conscious of what was involved in the suffering. It still happened, it caused suffering, I still feel terrible about it, but this is how I can live my life, how I can still wake up in the morning and not have to shed tears every day for Blue and Belle and all those animals whose lives I interrupted. I didn't know it then; I couldn't know it. I wish that someone had been an advocate for me. Maybe they could have progressed my animal advocacy; maybe they would have helped me to stop. The worse part about 4-H is that they teach you to make friends with this animal and then you kill it. If you can grow up killing your friend, what do you care about the cow in the supermarket? What do you care about the chicken at KFC?"

Kelley went on: "And of course, we know that the 4-H started the animal component because they wanted to make factory farming more palatable to the people who were raising food animals. After World War II, extension services spent a great deal of money finding new ways to increase farming productivity. But farmers were slow to implement the 'new technology.' The solution was to teach the 'farm kids' the new methods so that when they took over the 'family farm' they would be more comfortable with implementing the 'new and improved' farming methods and practices. They wanted to desensitize them to the feelings and pain of animals so that they would be more amenable to factory farms. This is why they started teaching kids to ignore the animals' pain. Looking at this reasoning as a humane educator today, I see this premise as a nightmare! We know now that there is a strong link between animal cruelty and violence to people. In light of that, teaching kids to kill their lamb, their pig, their best non-human friend whom they love, may not be such a great idea.

"The hardest thing for me was knowing that the reason

why I did the program is because I love animals. I don't get it—nobody gets it! I loved animals since the time I can remember. I used to sleep in the pasture with my cow Rosie, I took naps with her. I used to sleep in the barns. So how could I have played a part in these animals' misery and their suffering and their death?"

I wondered if Kelley had any good memories of her time with 4-H. I know from speaking to other professionals and even other humane educators that 4-H does have much to offer kids, and Kelley agreed that 4-H has a lot to offer that is not animal-exploitative, and provides ideals and values that can be of great significance to kids growing up today.

"Oh yes," Kelley assured me, "4-H does some good. I had to get up and haul ten-gallon buckets of water, and cleaned stalls and moved bales of hay and grain, and all of that was good. I learned how to shear sheep and in doing so learned that they do have feelings; they like certain people. 4-H has sewing and photography and cooking and oratory contests. There are all kinds of wonderful, character-building components that they offer. There is leadership skills, bonding, teamwork. The adults are usually great role models and children have the opportunity to run meetings.

"The animal part of 4-H I cry over still. The other parts of 4-H are good, but I think there are other programs out there that are not based on measuring animals for meat."

I wondered whether the number of children enrolled in 4-H might be declining due to urbanization. Not so, says Dr. Allan Smith, 4-H National Program Leader. The number of children enrolled has tripled over the past ten years. In 1992 1,844,824 children in grades 1–12 were enrolled. In 2002, enrollment was 3,039,199. However, the animals involved are less likely to be large farm animals, and more apt to be rabbits, chickens and other small animals, because the enrolled population is now more urban and suburban.[11] Small consolation to the animals involved.

I later raised the question of the mixed messages sent by 4-H and other children's activities with MaryAnn Jones, who serves on the Florida Governor's Task Force on Domestic Violence, and who is a survivor of domestic violence and marital rape. She is the author of *Sweet Potato Pie: The Workbook*, used in many domestic violence programs to aid victims fleeing life-threatening abusive relationships. Dr. Jones has been a speaker at HSUS First Strike workshops, educating audiences about the link between animal cruelty and domestic violence. She is a pretty young African-American woman, quiet and dignified, who has traveled the world. Sitting down together one hot summer day at a crowded Italian restaurant, we talked about the grief children feel when they face death for the first time at an early age through the loss of an animal companion. What must it be like for them to be put in the position of having to facilitate the killing of their nonhuman friends?

"I think that can be very injurious to children," said Dr. Jones. "Like the mutton-busting event where the child is taught to tackle and bring down a baby lamb. Now, we know that there are people who eat lamb, but it is giving a very weird kind of message to attack a lamb violently for the sake of sport. I was in Pakistan, and they have these lambs outside in the front and they would kill the lamb and have a kind of kosher type of ceremony. I didn't see the lamb being killed but I knew that the lamb had been walking around the front earlier. What was striking was that there was so much respect for the life that they had taken. They killed it in a particular way. They weren't cruel to the animal beforehand. Even then,

I thought it was kind of peculiar that the kids would form a kind of attachment and then have to kill the animal.

"I don't know how they reconcile this on family farms, how they can slaughter them after living among them. Maybe they build some kind of layer of protection, they insulate themselves. This is what any of us do when we see people who we think are good do very bad things. We normalize it. Kids who see their moms get beat, they normalize it, but what is their choice? To just sit and cry all day and be sad about it. We model ourselves after what the adults do in our environment. [In] 'mutton busting' [and calf roping], the children are watching respected adults acting like this and the message is very injurious to them."

I reflected on my conversations with Kelley and Dr. Jones one day while I was strolling with my dog Tyrone on a heart trail near our home in Florida. As I thought about the institutionalized, systematic inculcation of insensitivity through programs for children, I was reminded that organized children's activities represent only some of the ways in which children are being taught to disregard the feelings of animals. Individuals may be unintentionally teaching their children this very same lesson, one child at a time.

There is a duck pond in the middle of the heart trail where beautiful ducks and geese make their home. As I walked the trail with Tyrone, I saw a woman in a Cub Scout leader's uniform with two children. One of the children, a boy about ten years old, was stomping at and chasing the ducks and geese. I approached the group and watched for a minute. "Look at all the ducks!" the boy shouted to me. "Yes," I said, "but this is their home and you are scaring them. How would you like it if someone came into your home and frightened you?" The boy stopped cold and I could almost see the light bulb over his head. The scout leader challenged me, however, obviously upset that I had chastised her son. "It's just a little friendly exercise!" she said. I explained that this is how animal cruelty starts, and that as parents and leaders we have a responsibility to teach our children to respect all living things. "You fish, don't you?" she asked me. I don't fish, and her assumption that I did, that everyone did, helped me to understand that this boy was learning from his own mother that animals do not have feelings, cannot feel pain—not fish, not ducks, not any animal.

If this child's mother allowed him to chase ducks, where did she draw the line? Chase ducks but don't throw rocks? Throw rocks but don't shoot? Shoot ducks but not cats? Shoot cats but not dogs? How does a child discern this message?

How can we teach students that dog fighting is immoral and illegal, unethical and abhorrent, if we also teach them that tricking an animal into loving you, trusting you and living only for the moments she can be with you, when all along you know you are going to betray her, is not only all right but may win you a ribbon at the fair? How can we teach children not to bully smaller children when we also teach them that it is perfectly fine to terrorize ducks in a park? I asked this question of Dr. Jones. She explained,

"We say things like 'Don't hit your sister' but what is implied is 'Don't hit your sister even though I hit your mother.' The message is that in certain situations it is acceptable to overpower and hurt something that is more vulnerable than you are as a way to alter behavior or because you think that you are entitled to do that. Maybe this is why we are such a violent society. These are the messages. We do things because this is what we see; we don't question. I have a good friend who grew up on a farm. He is expected to follow a code of ethics, like an oath, a farmer's oath of some kind, that he will not harm the animals; he will uphold the profession and so on. But how do they reconcile that with pig gestation crates? It seems contradictory."

Indeed.

Yet, she reflects, "We see what we want to see. Like if you grow up with animals chained up all the time, you don't even have room to look at it a different way. You see it because that is the way animal interaction has been with the family you grew up with."

Dr. Randall Lockwood, Ph.D., of HSUS, believes that humane educators may be the only voice some children ever hear in favor of animals. "Children begin to abuse animals around the age of seven," says Dr. Lockwood, "And most children learn from their parents that this is wrong, that they should stop doing that. But some children never hear this message at home. They never hear it from respected adults; it just does not come up. Then they go to school and there is a visit from a humane educator and they hear for the first time that cruelty to animals is wrong. We have no idea what the impact on society is for humane educators to be able to relay this message. Maybe the serial killers who we know have had a history of animal abuse never heard that message. We don't know how many future violent criminals we stop when we teach them about compassion for animals. Being a humane educator is vitally important work in our society."

This is especially true when the humane message is challenged in the schools themselves. Rodeos, circuses, farms, 4-H and other animal-exploitative industries are relentless in their messages to children that it is perfectly acceptable to hurt and kill animals. But the Future Farmers of America

(FFA) goes further by spreading the same message in some schools with the permission of parents, teachers and the federal government, says author Kim Sturla, co-founder and director of Animal Place Sanctuary in California. "The FFA is a much bigger force to be reckoned with than 4-H, because they are funded with federal dollars. And, unlike 4-H, which is outside the school setting, it is integrated into the school curriculum. Through FFA, in many areas the animals are slaughtered right at the school site and the child is responsible for ending the project by walking the animal to the slaughter point and watching as the butcher kills him or her."

She shared one student's story with me: "Mindy was a student at a high school in San Jose, California. She was there when a local farming outfit donated live turkeys to the school. As she tells the story, the students were taken on a field trip with their turkeys in tow up to the slaughter plant, which was about an hour and half from the school. The birds were slaughtered while the students observed, and they all got their dead birds back to take home to eat. With mammals, the butcher comes to the school site with a box of donuts and the child is expected to walk their animal to the slaughter ring to have their animal killed. Mindy had raised a steer and she flipped out and tried not to get the animal slaughtered. But she was ostracized because she was emotional and sensitive and did not want to see the animal slaughtered."

Kim is concerned about the systematic desensitization to pain and suffering of programs like this one, as well as the exposure to violence, the betrayal of an animal's trust, and the valuing of profit over compassion. These practices, she says, represent the antithesis of what humane educators are trying to do. From every direction, children get the message that animals are to be exploited and treated as objects.

"There is this great video that the California egg board has," Kim tells me. "It's brilliant . . . a little girl is sitting on the green grass holding this little yellow chick. The scene changes as the chick grows. The thing is, it is not even a white leghorn, which is what they all use for egg laying in California; it's another breed altogether. It's a beautiful black and white speckled bird, and in each scene the little girl is sitting on this grass holding this bird as she grows up and the bird is growing up. And then the next scene is of a big semi truck delivering eggs for USDA inspection. You don't see the battery cages, the de-beaking, the culling of the male birds. You don't see any of that. You only see the USDA inspection and the message is that the USDA is meticulous in their inspection. Just by omission it is very well done. This is sanitizing at its best!"

Truly, humane educators have their work cut out for them as they help to rebuild bridges between children and animals. This is important work that we do. We have prejudices and biases and prevailing attitudes to overcome. But overcome them we must; the experts tell us so.

3

Getting Started

"Humane education should begin in the home as early as possible, and the formal kind of humane education should begin right away at the primary level. It should be part of the curriculum at every level and should continue as any other character education and development should continue throughout the learning years."

—Lt. Sherry Schlueter

As the previous chapter and our own experience tell us, we don't need to teach children to love animals! They are born with a natural affinity and affection for animals that can either grow in time or erode with each new adult who comes into their lives with not-so-friendly attitudes about animals. Our goal, as humane educators, is to foster that affection, encourage it and guide children towards making more humane choices as they grow into responsible adults. We are simply developing this innate connection with animals and teaching students why it is so important to them, to the environment and to the animals to treat them with compassion and respect. We do this not only for the sake of the animals, but for the sake of the children and the society in which they live.

Opportunities to teach your own children about beneficial choices are everywhere. While watching television, discuss the products in the commercials. Does the product harm the environment? If so, how is it harmful? Is there a similar product that would make a better choice? Is the product cruelty-free? How would you find out?

While visiting stores and shops in your community, point out which consumer choices are humane and which ones are not. If you purchase shade-grown coffee, for example, explain what you are doing and how it saves the rainforest; if a certain company donates money to charity and you purchase their products, be sure and tell your kids what you are doing and why. If there is someone outside the grocery store offering to give away a box full of puppies, ask your kids what may become of those puppies, what the person could have done instead and why his or her decision to hand out puppies to strangers may not be in the puppies' best interest.

If you take your kids to the movies, be ever cognizant of the surroundings and what products are being marketed—and, of course, the message the films are promoting. The movies *Snow Dogs*, *101 Dalmatians* and *Finding Nemo* did a terrible disservice to Siberian Huskies, Dalmatian dogs and Clownfish by creating a market for them. If you see previews or posters for movies such as these, be sure to open a discussion about how these movies, and others like them, generate a massive demand for animals who are then bred at an alarming rate and in deplorable conditions to meet the demand, only to end up in shelters soon after because the novelty has worn off. Interestingly, although *Finding Nemo* did create a market for Clownfish and is putting money in the pockets of pet stores that sell these fish and their suppliers, the overall message of *Finding Nemo* was that fish have lives of their own and that they don't like human interference. You can use products like these to open a discussion about the pros and cons of the messages that these movies, and others like them, convey.

Other movies, such as *Babe* and *Stuart Little*, *Chicken Run* and *Doctor Doolittle*, help us help children to make the connection between animals and ourselves. While never intended as humane education tools, these films perform beautifully in that role. Consider the case of *Babe*. When the movie opens, we see small piglets, cute as can be, become orphaned as their moms are sent to slaughter. Little minds presented with this scene can't help thinking about how the piglets must feel at the loss of their mother. How would any of us feel? In the movie *Chicken Run*, we see a lovable character trying valiantly to save herself and her friends from becoming chicken pot pies. Kids seeing this situation and putting themselves in the place of the animal about to die cannot help but feel a sense of kinship with that animal. Humane educators, hoping to help children make the connection between the animals in the movies and the animals on their plates, have found a valuable resource in these films.

If you are a parent who is teaching your own children about animals, or are home schooling or caring for children in a home environment, you can also make use of television, videos or the Internet. There are scores of videos available for children of all ages that can be purchased for a reasonable fee. Animal Planet, while not always the most animal-friendly channel on television, does offer several pro-animal programs such as *Animal Cops*, *Animal ER* and *Animal Precinct* that depict professionals working to save animal lives and mete out justice for animal abusers. These programs are more appropriate for middle and high schoolers, but the Internet offers educational websites where children of all ages can participate in "cyber hunts" to learn about all kinds of animal issues, from preventing fleas to passing legislation to make life better for animals. Learn to separate the wheat from the chaff when searching for lessons. Lesson plans, videos, and books may be found among some not-so-animal-friendly sources, but take what you need and leave the rest.

It's easy to incorporate humane education into your day-to-day interactions with your own children. But what about taking that to the next level and offering to teach a humane education lesson to your first-grader's classmates or your middle-schooler's after-care club? That takes a little more creativity, initiative and planning.

If you are a parent, simply ask your child's teacher if you may present an age-appropriate lesson (from this book or one of the sources mentioned below or in the appendix) in your child's grade, or find a local Delta Society chapter to see if experienced humane educators and their assistance dogs are available. If you do not work with a humane society, perhaps your veterinarian would help sponsor a humane education program through his or her clinic. This method of giving back to the community would make for great public relations for the veterinarian's practice and may also help you with funding for materials such as photocopies, overhead transparencies and books.

Use lessons that are very mainstream, non-controversial and educational. You can order lesson plans, literature and materials from any of the national organizations, such as the Humane Society of the United States (HSUS) or the American Humane Association (AHA), or you can develop them yourself with a little creativity and enthusiasm. It's fun to put together your own campaign to show to teachers, administrators and others whose support you wish to elicit. You may decide to use the lesson plans and ideas from the national organizations, but make the programs uniquely your own, with your own mascots, characters, slogans and buzzwords.

Catchy characters are not only useful for "selling" humane education to children but can also help make your program attractive to a teacher or principal. Who among us cannot identify a big purple dinosaur named Barney or a fussy little she-pig named Miss Piggy? How about Kermit the Frog or Clifford the Big Red Dog? Pound Puppies, Sagwa the Siamese cat, Winnie the Pooh, Garfield, Snoopy, Smokey the Bear—the list goes on and on. What they all have in common, of course, is that they are all animals that appeal, in a very big way, to children (and not a few adults!) Animal characters have been capturing children's imaginations since the first toy made its debut, and big corporations have been following suit ever since. If McDonalds can use miniature bean bag animals and a pig named Babe to sell hamburgers, then surely we can use animals to find our way into the hearts and minds of American children so that we can teach them about compassion, respect and reverence for all living creatures. Creating catchy characters based on real-life animals is a fun and lighthearted way to teach children about companion-animal responsibility and other animal issues.

Take Woody, for example. Woody is the real-life yellow Lab who accompanies me to classrooms and hospitals. But on the brochures used to advertise the program, she is depicted as a cartoon. She is larger than life, friendly, welcoming and fun. Studies show that characters such as Woody appeal to both males and females, ages three to seven, the exact audience for the lessons advertised in the brochure.

If you want to give birth and life to the next Tony the Tiger, it's important to know your target audience. Different characters, ideas and methods will appeal to different demographics. Here are some suggestions for developing your program:

If you are looking to appeal to students in kindergarten through second grade, go for characters that are whimsical, colorful and full of fantasy. This is the age where anything goes. All things magic, enchanting and fanciful are the winners in this age group. Your mascots can be anything from dinosaurs to talking cats. The more colorful and outlandish your characters are, the better. The characters at this level can afford to be funny and playful because we are not discussing life-and-death issues here. We are only teaching about the basics of animal care, the treatment animals need and deserve, why we should value animals, how to treat them as we want to be treated and how to show them love and respect.

If your target audience is grades three through six, then you need to rein in your creativity just a little. Students in these grades are quickly and fiercely moving away from anything "babyish" and looking for ways to find their place in the world. They are interested in sequential thinking (if this, then that), so this is the group where we first broach the subject of spaying and neutering, overpopulation and the consequences. We do so delicately, of course, because the subject, the death of unwanted puppies and kittens, is so very difficult to talk about. Your characters should be hip, sympathetic and very cool—think N'Sync or even Bart Simpson.

For grades seven through twelve, stay away from invented characters and find sports figures, celebrities and/or heroes who are animal-oriented and actively working to help animals. Watch for little things that celebrities do to help animals and use their examples. When Bill Goldberg, a World Wrestling Federation celebrity, publicly spoke out against dog and cock fighting, humane educators around the country ordered posters with his picture on it declaring that he does not believe in animals fighting for their lives. Boys wanting to emulate him (and there were a lot of them) heard his message loud and clear. Vegan actress Alicia Silverstone, who starred in *Clueless* and *Batman and Robin*, is another effective role model and animal-rights spokesperson. I like to show students my most prized possession, a photo of myself with NBA star Charles Barkley, and explain that working for animals brings with it some wonderful benefits. I met "Sir Charles" at an Animal Rights Foundation of Florida anniversary dinner where he appeared with several of his teammates, including Clyde Drexler. The moment the photo appears on the overhead projection never fails to bring gasps of delight and recognition, along with cries of "Is that you?" and "That's Charles Barkley!" Again, the national organizations have all kinds of posters, videos and public service announcements available using celebrity spokespersons. At this grade level we are discussing careers in working with animals, activism in its many forms, political action to help animals, how animals enhance our lives, overpopulation issues, dog/cat bite prevention techniques, zoonoses (diseases common to both human and non-human animals) and environmental considerations.

To understand the process of getting a program approved through your school system you must first be familiar with the lessons and the goals they seek to meet. You will read more about lesson plans and educational materials in chapter seven. Each lesson plan has a specific objective that students should be able to recognize and repeat at the conclusion of your presentation, and you can meet each lesson's goals even if you are not an animal expert. For example, if you are teaching a class about animal communication (dog bite prevention) and how to recognize when a dog is communicating to you that he or she is fearful or unhappy, angry or threatened, your students should be able to identify at least three signs that a dog is about to bite (e.g., ears alert and forward, tail tucked or flagging, teeth bared). They should be able to identify three things they should or should not do (e.g., never stare into a dog's eyes, never run, and offer the dog something to bite, such as a book or backpack). In order to teach these lessons, one need only be able to impart the knowledge in a fun, creative and interactive manner.

Have a good time with this and remember that no matter what lessons you are hoping to teach, if you cannot grab the attention of teachers and students, you won't get your message heard. So whether your choices include well-known and well-loved characters, new characters you develop yourself or celebrity spokespersons, breathe life into your lesson plans with style and excitement.

When you have developed your program, organize your

plans into a binder and make an appointment to visit your local school district headquarters. Some investigative phone calls should bring you to exactly the right person who has the authority to give you permission to enter the schools. You should also check with after-school programs, dropout prevention programs, and other alternative-educational programs. You will find that these are your strongest allies in getting your messages to the students because they are focused on keeping the children in school and teaching them life skills such as compassion and empathy, as opposed to just academic skills such as reading, writing and math. Most schools have a district-wide newsletter that goes out to all the teachers. Inquire as to how you may advertise your program in this publication, or ask if you can write a story for the newsletter about the program you are offering.

The following chapters will present lesson plans and discuss the use of animals in humane education. Before we embark on these important topics, here are some tips to help you stay focused and insure that you will be welcomed back again and again:

- Bring your own materials whenever possible. This means overhead transparencies (you can use the teacher's projector, television or VCR), markers and any handouts. Many times teachers have to use their own money to purchase supplies such as markers or transparencies, so try not to ask to use them if possible.
- Bring an extension cord if you have a Power Point projector or other electric device (such as a laptop or microscope).
- Bring plastic baggies for scooping if your dog needs to relieve himself or herself. This is best done before you

arrive at the school, but nature can't always follow a script!

- Bring name tags for yourself and any volunteers or observers you may have with you. You can make one for yourself or ask the humane society volunteer coordinator for one.
- Dress professionally but not do not overdress. Most teachers wear blue jeans with tailored blouses or shirts. This is appropriate because many times you will be seated on the floor or even on the grass. Try not to wear skirts, dresses or pantyhose because you never know whether you will be standing in a classroom or outside on the lawn, sitting in a circle.
- Bring bottled water for yourself and a bowl for your canine companion. Set a good example by offering your dog a drink both before and after the class. Make sure the students see that you are doing so.
- Bring literature on the shelter or veterinary clinic that you are representing or any pamphlets that are relevant to your lesson. You may find an abundance of this type of literature online.
- Keep an open and friendly attitude.

Finally, make sure the regular classroom teacher is always close at hand. Penny Milkins, a Florida humane educator who is also a certified teacher, works in a classroom of at-risk kids in an elementary school. She offers this story about what happened in one third-grade class as a warning that humane lessons don't always bring out the humaneness in students. "I was showing a CD Rom program about whales. I had my laptop set up and we were watching these Orcas when suddenly one kid turned to the other and said, 'Looks like your mama!' Well the two of them started fighting and I had to grab my equipment because it was going to get knocked over in the chaos, and it was just pandemonium!" So keep the teacher close by, because you never know what challenges may arise!

Being the local animal expert is not as difficult as it seems. If you have clear lesson plans with goals and objectives, it is not necessary to have a full and complete knowledge of all things animal. You can always write down questions that you don't know the answer to, research them, and get back to a student. Do this enough times, and you will soon become an expert. Learn from veterinarians, books and the Internet. You can start with a few good books about animals (there is a bibliography in the back of the book to help you get started), and supplement your knowledge as time goes on. Avail yourself of every opportunity to attend workshops, seminars or lectures about animals. Learn, then let others fill their cup from your pitcher of knowledge. I used to say that there is nothing more rewarding than speaking up for those who cannot speak for themselves. But now I know that there is something far more rewarding than that, teaching others to speak up for those who cannot speak for themselves. You won't believe how good you will feel at the end of a day of teaching others to care about animals.

4

Evaluating Your Partners

"When paws touch hands in friendship, hearts are touched with joy."

—Michelle Rivera

Not all humane educators include animals in their presentations, for reasons discussed at greater length in the next chapter. And not all animals are suited to working in a classroom environment. This chapter is for those humane educators who are interested in bringing animals into the classroom, to help you find the right animal to incorporate into your program.

I was lucky to be able to start my career in humane education with two of the best partners anyone could ask: Woody and Katie. Woody is ten years old and small for a Labrador. She is a most happy and energetic dog, though age has slowed her somewhat and she walks with a slight limp, perhaps the first signs of arthritis. Woody (named for Woody Herman and the Woodchoppers, a jazz band from the forties) takes to snapping the air when she is happy, and bounces on all fours when her joy can't be contained. Her sister is eleven-year-old Katie, an Australian shepherd with eyes the color of molasses and a disposition to match: loving, affectionate and sweet to a fault. She is a true beauty, with piercing eyes that can see into your very soul. Woody and Katie are the companion animals of two talented and altruistic veterinarians, Lisa Degen and Mike Berkenblit, whom they accompany every day to work. It was there, at Village Animal Clinic, while working as a veterinary technician, that I first met these irrepressible dogs and began taking them to hospice.

But our journey has taken a different route, and now instead of visiting those about to pass over and who need only solace and comforting, we enter the noisy world of children and teachers, books and classrooms, school boards and mandates. It was a challenge we took on with great anticipation. Woody and Katie loved being with kids and could hardly restrain their joy when they began to figure out where they were going when they saw me come to the clinic.

"Going with a dog or an animal has a particular dimension that adds a great deal to the program," says Ann Gearhart, a former teacher and now a humane educator with the Snyder Foundation for Animals. "For many of the children, they probably don't remember a fact that I recite, but they have a visual image and they internalize something about the dog. It's not just the dog, it's you and the dog. It's the relationship. You can then say, 'Should we use this dog for bait to teach pit bulls how to fight?' and they say, 'NO!' They react that way because in just a few minutes they have already bonded with the dog. There is a dimension, a face, a presence. This is what we are going out to do and that is what we can't assess or evaluate. There is no tool for assessing that. There is no quantitative result."

She adds, "I sometimes get so aggravated when I go to a school and people will see me with this dog. She's thirty-five pounds and wears a blue vest. How many times a day do you see a dog wearing a vest with words on it 'Activity Dog'? Yet there I am at a school, and some kid will come around the corner and scream like they just saw Dracula's incarnation. It's so annoying to me because they are so dramatic. They are so out of control. They can say or do anything they want. There is a lack of decorum. There is a lack of respect for authority. Then we get into the classroom and the teacher admonishes them to have respect for the dog, for me. There's another lesson in character development."

Finally, Ann says, "What [children] see in the relationship I have with that dog transcends anything I may say about having a dog. It is a big deal for a child who is terrified of dogs because of chained dogs or dog fighting in their neighborhood to actually reach out, with a shaking hand, and touch a dog. That is a transcendent moment for a child. I wish I could spend more time with that child, but even that moment is enough."

Mitch Sigal, of the Society of Prevention of Cruelty to Animals in Los Angeles (SPCA LA), says "I love having an animal in the classroom presentation. I feel that it is what makes the biggest impact on the kids. In fact, at SPCA LA, we have brought to classes various types of animals, including dogs, cats, rabbits, reptiles, etc. We have to, since we are frequently asked to come back to a school multiple times. There are some classes that do not want an animal, but that is a very small percentage. Most of my volunteers also use animals in their presentations. Either they have their own animal or they use one of ours.

"Every domestic animal must be safe and pass a rigorous temperament test before going into a school. We stand firm that there are no exceptions, because one bad experience can ruin the entire program. We take great pride in the fact that all of our animals have been tested and passed [SPCA LA uses a variation of a program developed by canine expert Sue Sternberg], and that SPCA LA also carries insurance for the educators and the animals. I do have one volunteer who does not use any animals, but her presence alone is incredible and she does fine without an animal. . . . When it comes to reptiles, I have specific staff and volunteers who have expertise with the critters, and only safe ones are brought into the class with my consent and the school's first." After all, Mitch explains, "Dogs and cats are not the only animals that kids will come into contact with. There is a large wildlife population here in Southern California."

Mitch has a point . . . but what about horses? I first met Margaret when she answered an ad I had placed in the local newspaper in an effort to recruit new volunteer animal-facilitated therapists or humane educators:

> *If you have a friendly companion animal that you would like to work with (as long as your companion animal isn't an enormous tarantula), please join us at an orientation meeting to learn how you and your companion can team up for education.*

I anticipated the usual suspects, people who had lovely dogs and cats, perhaps a ferret, a pet snake, a parrot or a rabbit. I was unprepared for the companion animal Margaret had in store for me.

"He's a horse," she explained when it came her turn to introduce herself and talk about her animal. "Oh, okay," I said, "Like in horses for the handicapped?" I was thinking about the wonderful horses whose services have been used to help emotionally handicapped children.

"Not exactly," said Margaret. ""He's a mini."

"A mini?" She had my attention and was clearly enjoying the curious looks from the others in the room, who had proudly stood up and told loving stories about their poodles, collies and Bichons. This lady had outdone them all!

"Yes, well, he's only 38 inches high and weighs in at about 185 pounds. He's very friendly, and he's just perfect for little kids." So when I wrote to all the nursing homes and hospitals, schools and children's advocacy groups about our program, the list of new therapy animals we had to offer included a miniature horse named Teddy.

Claire, the activities director at the Jupiter Medical Center Pavilion, a rehabilitation center, was the first inquiring person to call. "So, about this horse?" she asked.

"Well, I only met him myself a few days ago, but if you would like, we can give it a try," I said, confident that Teddy would be great. When Margaret had brought him to our shelter to meet us a few days before, on April 1, my first reaction had been disbelief. How, I wondered, could an animal as magnificent and awesome as a horse be compacted into something the size of a large dog? Yet, here he was, in the flesh. It wasn't that I had never seen a miniature horse . . . it was just that I had never been so close to one! After fussing over him a little, and seeing how well behaved and teeny-tiny he was, I decided bring him indoors to meet the shelter staff.

Being that it was April Fools Day (and me not one to let an opportunity like this pass by), we led him into the "lost and found" area and pronounced that he was a foundling we were turning in. May, a veteran shelter worker who had the air of one who had seen one too many tragedies in her lifetime, raised her eyebrows slightly and with a deep sigh said "Okay." When word of Teddy's presence spread, the rest of the staff piled into the "lost and found" area to see him. Teddy's visit was a nice break from the deeply saddening tasks that comprise a day in the life of a shelter worker. Thus, Teddy was performing his first act of animal-assisted therapy: ministering to the euthanasia technicians, the crematorium workers and the vets and kennel staff, who always are in need of some diversion and tender loving concern. Teddy, with his sweet and gentle nature, was the perfect therapist.

I explained all this to Claire, who was eagerly waiting to set up a visit with Teddy and the residents of the nursing home. "Oh, let's do it," said Claire. "We have a lot of visitors with therapy dogs, a few with kittens, but something different would be really nice."

So I met Margaret in the medical center's parking lot a few days later, and together we untied the braid Margaret had carefully placed in Teddy's tail to keep it from sweeping the sawdust and hay in his horse trailer. The Pavilion was all a-titter over the presence of their equine visitor, and soon people with walkers and oxygen tanks and nurses' aides wheeling patients all gathered in the butterfly garden. It was a beautiful moment, but the hot Florida sun soon drove us all back inside. Teddy was invited in as well, and he clearly enjoyed being in the air conditioning. As we traveled from room to room, escorting little Teddy around the facility, the word spread to the adjoining hospital, and soon nurses and doctors had made their way over to see the little horse with the big, big heart.

This was our foray into the world of animal-assisted therapy involving this sweet little horse, but it certainly wasn't our last. It served as an excellent introduction into our humane education program as Teddy made his way around classrooms and kids' clubs all over the county! One day, we even walked him down a street in a run-down, crack-infested neighborhood, delighting kids and their grandmas, who could not get over the sight of a miniature horse trotting across their front lawn. This little stroll attracted the attention of our local NBC affiliate, who later did a segment on Teddy and his special brand of therapy for the six o'clock news!

Teddy is the embodiment of what animal-assisted therapy and humane education activity animals stand for. The Delta Society is one of the organizations that set the standards for these animals. A Seattle-based nonprofit organization that screens animals for personality, obedience and temperament, the Delta Society helps facilitate the animal–human bond every day by insuring that the animals that are being included in animal-assisted activities and classroom presentations are fully qualified. This means that they are tolerant, easygoing, gentle and, perhaps most of all, enjoy working with people.

Remember, if you decide to include an animal in your humane education programs, be sure that he or she is well suited for working with children. The first step is always to make sure the animal has a good steady temperament, is not easily startled and can follow basic instructions—and that you can read him or her well enough to detect signs of stress that would signal you to remove him or her from the situation. No matter how much you want to work with your companion, it is not worth a child being bitten by a frightened animal. There are several organizations such as Delta that will help you evaluate your chosen animal for assistance work.

When I called our local Delta Society evaluators to meet with my volunteers, I had already been bringing animals into classrooms for nearly six years—animals I thought fit the above description very well! However, I always felt uneasy knowing that the animals themselves had not been fully and professionally evaluated. My experience with bringing Woody and Katie into the classroom was a little more comfortable because I had full confidence in their ability to interact with the children and consistently behave suitably. Their distinctive green vests, earned through the Delta certification, made them singular. I wanted each of the animals we employed in our programs to be similarly tested and registered. In short, I wanted "bragging rights"! I felt that the teachers would appreciate that extra measure of assurance as well.[12]

I had eleven eager volunteers, each with "the world's best" dog or cat. All the volunteers believed with all their hearts that their dog or cat would ace the evaluation and go on to a brilliant career in humane education, spreading sunshine throughout the land. Of the eleven animals who came to the evaluation, two passed. As each animal failed parts of the test, we all felt the disappointment. We sincerely wanted these animals to play a part in humane education, and we wanted their guardians to be proud of them. The evaluation proved that not every dog and cat is cut out of animal-assisted activity cloth. And indeed, after some discussion, the animals who failed the evaluation did not continue their work with me in classrooms, because we felt that they did not enjoy the work. They just were not the kind of animals that liked their routines upset and discovering new things.

As you read through the steps of a Delta evaluation, outlined below, try to imagine what your dog, or your volunteer's dog, might do in these situations. In our group, from the German shepherd who nipped at the evaluator when she tried to brush him to the cat who climbed up on her mom's shoulders in an effort to avoid people, the candidates fell away at different stages. Some made it through the primary levels only to lose their way near the end of the evaluation. Don't be disheartened if your beloved animal companion doesn't get through all the steps. He or she is still the best dog or cat in the world!

The dogs are brought into a room with the evaluators—in our case, Maureen Parsons and Karen Frick of the Sunshine on a Leash Club in Jupiter, Florida.[13] Along with Maureen and Karen are several volunteers who are asked to perform certain tasks throughout the evaluation. Behind a closed door somewhere in the room is a strange dog, whom Delta refers to as a "neutral" dog, to be brought out later in the session. In our case, sweet Woody was the neutral dog.

The dogs must have basic obedience skills. The handlers are asked to imagine a box around themselves and the dog, outside which the dog is not allowed to venture. If he does, the evaluation is abruptly over. He must stay close and in control. This "box" proved to cause trouble for a lot of our candidates. We overheard one person muttering to her companion as they left after failing that step "That's an awfully small box they gave us!" Smaller dogs may be carried if they can be picked up with one hand, and can be offered for petting either in a basket or in a blanket. Cats, rabbits, ferrets, rats, guinea pigs and the like are held in this fashion as well. The dog's handler and the evaluator meet and shake hands, and the dog's reaction to this encounter with a stranger is noted. In our evaluation, Maureen did the actual interaction while Karen noted the dog's reactions. The next step brings Maureen to the dog with a grooming brush to see how well that is tolerated. If the dog tolerates this well, she moves on to the next step.

At this stage, the dog must be put through some basic commands. He or she must be able to sit, lie down, stay, come and walk on a loose leash. The animal may be coached gently; that is, the handler may gently encourage the dog to perform these commands if he or she doesn't do so immediately. It's not an obedience show where the candidates are earning points for obedience. One of the volunteers asked if the dogs all had their CDs, meaning their "Companion Dog" title, a title given to exceptionally trained, well-behaved dogs. Maureen said that although they encourage well-trained dogs, they do not insist on the dog having an obedience title, because they don't want the dogs to be so trained that they do whatever they are told without thinking for themselves. The evaluators want to be able to determine whether the dogs are actually enjoying the work or if they are only performing for their guardians. I love the idea that part of the Delta evaluation is insuring that the animal is enjoying interactions with people. They are not just looking for well-behaved or even well-trained dogs and cats, but also dogs and cats who like people. This single requirement, by the way, is what knocked my own Tyrone, a fine, upstanding Standard Poodle, out of the running. This is why I have to go dog-begging, because my own dog would never enjoy going to classrooms and being with kids. He's a nervous wreck, and that makes me a nervous wreck. Recognizing this in your own beloved animal companion who can do no wrong is difficult, and Maureen and Karen find that convincing a dog or cat guardian that his or her beloved angel is unfit for therapy or assistance work is difficult at best.

Before the skills testing is over, the dogs are led past Woody, the neutral dog. They may show a mild interest, but they cannot jump up and spin in circles or, heaven forbid, growl or snarl at her.

If they make it through their basic obedience tests, the real fun starts. They are put through a series of trials such as being lightly petted, then heavily petted, then hugged, exposed to a loud argument (this is where the volunteers come in), being approached by someone who is stumbling around, someone else in a wheelchair and/or someone with a walker making all kinds of noise. A bedpan is dropped somewhere nearby to see if they are jumpy at loud noises, and finally, they are asked to walk by a toy on the ground without too much fuss. They are offered a treat, which they must take gently from Maureen's hand. The cats are also subjected to these tests (with the exception of staying in the box while going through obedience commands) and must stay unruffled, composed and quite calm throughout the ordeal. Small dogs and cats are passed around from one "patient" or student to the next.

Many of the dogs made it through so many of the levels that when they failed towards the end of the evaluation it was a disappointment to all. One dog, a favorite of mine called Emmy who had already been accompanying me to classrooms, was a lovable "Goofy" look alike. She was sweet to the kids and a real pleasure to be around. But when she saw Woody, the wolf in her came out and she surprised us all with her ferocity! "Where did that come from?" we wondered. She was fine with strange dogs in the neighborhood! How could this have happened? It was enough to fail the test, and nobody was more disappointed than Maureen and Karen, because Emmy had been such a favorite among our volunteers. Her guardian took it hard and felt confused and betrayed by Emmy's behavior.

But then, Essence took the floor. Essence is the largest and most beautiful Rottweiler that I have ever seen. She is the quintessential gentle giant, with a sweet, benevolent soul. Essence went through her paces with charm and skill, adroitly showing her obedience skills, benignly taking in all the noise and fuss and primly nodding at Woody like a queen. She was amazing, and for those of us who were witnessing this evaluation and had seen the others throughout the day, it finally became clear to us what being a Delta Dog meant. Charm, elegance, goodness and love—Essence had it all. Her guardian, Julia, a former Rottie breeder, was an expert on all things "dog." Essence and Julia became a valuable and welcome addition to my humane education programs. The other dog who passed that day was a beauty named Cassie, a sweet little Bichon who had failed an earlier evaluation. This time, Cassie passed with flying colors, and her mom, Sheree, practically exuded pride. Cassie, too, had been working with me with elementary schoolchildren and had done very well.

I encourage those considering implementing a humane education program to visit www.DeltaSociety.org and learn more about their philosophies, programs and services. Cassie and Essence, just like Woody and Katie and thousands of other dogs before them, now proudly wear their green Delta Society vests wherever they go. They earned them, and that says a lot.

5

Canines in the Classroom

"From the earliest of times, animals have accompanied us on a journey that has been both disturbing and rewarding."

—Ann Gearhart, Humane Educator

As discussed in chapter four, many humane educators feel that the inclusion of animals in a humane education program makes for an exciting and interactive program. There are those educators who feel otherwise, and their reasons for excluding animals from their presentations are as varied as the educators themselves. The prevailing reasons run the gamut from "It's too distracting" to "I don't feel that animals should be used for our purposes, including humane education." The most important thing is to do what feels right and comfortable for you. This is because if you are not comfortable with having an animal accompany you, your attitude will reflect that and the children will pick up on your discomfort. More importantly, if you are not completely comfortable with your choice of animal—perhaps you take a shelter dog or a friend's dog who is "just great with kids," and you are not totally at ease with that animal—you will be nervous and anxious, and things won't go as well as they should. I have found this to be true on more than one occasion. Once, when I was determined to prove that pit bulls are lovely animals and to dispel the cruel myths that surround them, I jumped at the opportunity to bring a friend's female American Staffordshire "pit bull" terrier to an after-school presentation. The dog, while being exceptionally sweet-tempered and loving, was not well trained, and she pulled and tugged hard at the leash. Her anxiety at being in a room full of kids caused her to have a big, pungent accident on the floor of the library, which set the stage for a most uncomfortable session. I quickly learned that having a good temperament is only part of the equation when searching for a suitable assistance animal. The animal should be obedience trained, because we are trying to encourage good canine citizenship and need to set an ideal example. And he or she should be completely at ease in a setting where there are a lot of kids making a lot of noise. Bringing an animal to a classroom so that kids can pet him or her gives a mixed message if the animal is not clearly enjoying the attention. It makes little sense to try to teach children to have respect for all animals while we are visibly ignoring the feelings of the animal in our care.

Another controversy involves exotic pets. The inclusion of

exotic pets, such as reptiles, amphibians or other wild animals that have been domesticated, is never a good idea. The exotic pet trade in our country is a sham and a disgrace and should never be promoted by a humane educator.

According to the People for the Ethical Treatment of Animals (PETA), Americans are purchasing exotic animals such as hedgehogs, macaws, lizards and monkeys to keep as "pets." But captivity is often a death sentence for these animals, who frequently suffer inappropriate habitats or loss of nutrition, isolation, and the trauma of confinement. For every animal we find in the pet store or auction, incalculable others die along the way.

Even when birds and reptiles are legally purchased from pet shops or dealers, a brutal, illegal trade in exotic animals is being unwittingly supported. Birds, especially, face a cruel fate when smuggled into the United States. They are often force-fed and have their wings clipped and their beaks taped shut, and are packed into everything from spare tires to luggage. It's not unusual for eighty percent of the birds in one shipment to die. Reptiles are drugged and stuffed into containers with false bottoms, and many of them die in transit. Wildlife experts estimate that the illegal trade in exotic animals is a $10 billion-a-year business. Wild animals today, ounce for ounce, are worth more to smugglers than cocaine.

Taking animals from their natural habitats not only endangers individual animals—it endangers complete ecosystems. For example, the population of the South American hyacinth macaw has dropped seventy-five percent in the last ten years due to smugglers' capturing of the birds for U.S. and European collectors. In Argentina, trappers have cut down thousands of quebracho trees since 1976 to reach fledgling macaws in their nests, destroying the habitat for all the remaining animals.

Animals bred in captivity usually fare no better. For example, to help generate demand for pot-bellied pigs, breeders tell unsuspecting buyers that these animals won't grow beyond forty pounds. To keep pigs small, unscrupulous breeders may deprive the pigs of food or inbreed them. But once adopted, pigs often grow to two hundred pounds or more. Birds older than eight to ten weeks of age don't sell well at pet shops, so many are kept for breeding, confined to small, filthy cages. Nest boxes usually offer no means of escape, endangering female birds, who can be injured or killed by sexually aggressive males. One trade magazine warns that hedgehogs, which are growing in popularity as pets, become stressed from being confined, fed an improper diet, or forced to have too many litters, and may display erratic behavior, including deserting, or even eating, their babies.

There are also many hidden dangers to humans. Some exotic animals are regulated by laws that make it illegal for private individuals to keep them. These laws are usually designed not to protect animals, but to protect humans from animals who may be dangerous or who can carry transmittable diseases. For example, people can contract diseases like tuberculosis and hepatitis B from monkeys. Iguanas and other reptiles—the fastest-growing segment of the exotic animals trade—can and do transmit salmonella bacteria to humans. Animals such as raccoons and hedgehogs often suffer from distemper, mange, parasites, and bacterial and viral infections, which can be transferred to domestic animals.

Aside from the danger to humans, enormous suffering can also result from disregard or lack of knowledge when exotic animals are kept in captivity. For example, iguanas, extremely popular in the exotic-pet trade, can suffer debilitating illnesses—and death—if they are not provided with enough sunlight (for proper calcium metabolism) or if they are fed inadequate diets. Hedgehogs, who roll themselves into tight balls, can easily become injured when children try to "uncurl" them or if cats roll them across floors.

According to animal shelter sources, sixty percent of all wild animals who are kept as "pets" die within the first month of ownership; of the remainder, twenty percent die within the first year, and only ten percent are still alive by the end of the second year. People who decide later to "get rid" of their exotic pet typically have a very hard time finding a place that will take them. The American Zoo and Aquarium Association advises zoos to refuse exotic animals from people who are unable or unwilling to care for them. Jack Cover, a curator at the National Aquarium in Baltimore, says, "We'd have to have two or three warehouses to handle the donations we get calls on." Some people sneak animals into exhibits—and risk infecting zoo populations with diseases—or leave animals in front of zoo gates; usually these animals are euthanized. Others try to return unwanted animals to their natural homes—or simply abandon them along rural roads—but without appropriate rehabilitation, these animals will starve or fall victim to the elements or predators. Many pot-bellied pigs are taken to slaughterhouses when their owners tire of them.[14]

As humane educators, we do not want to unwittingly support the exotic pet trade. By bringing exotic animals into the classrooms, we may unintentionally give kids the idea that they can and should go out and purchase an exotic for themselves. No matter what we may be telling them, "Do as I say and not as I do" is an ineffective teaching method and just does not work.

The one exception that I indulge in is where snakes are

concerned. I began bringing Chance, a lovely little red rat snake (a.k.a. corn snake) into the classroom because I tired of hearing all the stories of hapless snakes being killed in backyards across America simply because they were in the wrong place at the wrong time. Invariably on my classroom visits, a kid will raise his or her hand and say a variation of the following: "My dad found a snake in the backyard and we killed it with a shovel!" This statement is delivered with a great deal of pride and satisfaction. My stock answer, "I am so sorry to hear that," is usually met with looks of confusion and chagrin. Then I go on to explain how snakes are performing a service to nature and that when you kill a snake you are robbing nature of that service. Sometimes the kids understand this concept, but more often they do not. It was not until I began bringing Chance to classrooms that the students and teachers began to understand how unnecessary it is to kill snakes in our backyards.

Corn snakes are among the most common and beautiful species native to the southeastern region of the United States. As such, they are found in gardens across Florida and are at risk for being killed just for "being." They are not poisonous snakes and pose no risk to humans. In fact, their presence in a backyard could very well indicate a rodent situation that they are keeping under control. Snakes won't stay where there is no food source, so the presence of a corn snake, or any snake, in the yard is cause for concern over a possible rat or mouse problem. If the snake is removed, the rodents will take over, often prompting homeowners to resort to inhumane and somewhat expensive measures.

This is a perfect humane education lesson because it speaks to a real situation kids face every day! I felt, however, that without seeing for themselves firsthand that snakes are not all dangerous or evil, the students would never completely trust or understand the message. It was important for me to find a red rat snake who was tame, but not a pet.

Not being a snake expert myself, I enlisted the aid of my friend David Hitzig of Busch Wildlife Sanctuary in Jupiter, Florida. He has a brilliant and talented snake expert on staff, Alyson Strange. Alyson is tall and thin with sunny blonde hair and a special affection for the most despised of all animals. I invited her to come and speak to one of my classes. She readily accepted and was pleased to bring her four-and-a-half-foot red rat snake. This little guy was a domesticated animal who had been found by a Good Samaritan one sunny South Florida day. At the time, he had a huge golf-ball sized lump on the end of his tail, and David and his vets determined that the tumor was cancerous. They removed the tumor and amputated part of his tail. "He is not a candidate for re-release, even though that is always our goal, because cancers come back and if that happens, we won't be able to help him a second time," explained Alyson. So this amazing little snake, (named Chance by a local elementary school class) is an ambassador for the reptile kingdom, helping children understand and respect snakes. After our initial visit Alyson trusted me to start taking Chance in on a regular basis, and, with a few lessons in snake husbandry from Alyson, I learned how to handle him and show him to schoolchildren in their classrooms.

The reaction to Chance's visit was always astounding. Some of the children were understandably nervous at the thought of a snake in their room, but for the most part the kids took to Chance like little fishes to water. I had to caution one child to stop trying to kiss Chance, because snakes can carry salmonella, and another child openly cried when he realized that the snake that had been killed in his backyard was a snake very much like Chance. The teachers, too, were amazed at how tame and "friendly" this little snake was, and we discussed his fate and how sad it is that the only guarantees in his life are that he will never be killed as long as he lives in captivity.

Note: It's important to reveal certain facts when you bring an appealing snake like Chance into a classroom, because children who like the snake may decide they want to adopt one of their own. For example, snakes require live food. This alone is enough of a turn-off to most people. Beyond that, many snakes can live to be thirty years old. Ten-, eleven- and twelve-year-olds are generally receptive to the suggestion that they can't really know how they will feel about living with that snake when they are in their forties, with kids and a job.

Sometimes, we can simply explain how beneficial snakes are, how friendly they can be and how they shouldn't be killed, and maybe the message will get through. But I believe that the message is much more powerful when delivered by the snake himself. I am certain that the children who survived their snake visit will look upon Chance's kin much differently the next time they are faced with a renegade snake in their backyard. Hopefully, they won't be so quick to take a shovel to the innocent creature! Of course, if you are not comfortable with snakes and cannot bear the thought of handling one, you may want to leave this particular lesson to the snake experts. Again, your comfort level with the animal is of paramount important.

Snakes are classified not only as exotic animals but also as wild animals. There are many wild animal traveling shows that take it upon themselves to visit classrooms under the Humane Education umbrella. But they may be doing more harm than good. When wild animals such as raccoons and opossums, squirrels and assorted wild birds are brought into the classroom, the message is clear: "See how I am handling this tame animal? See how he responds to me? You can have one, too!" Children get the impression that all wild animals can be domesticated, and they want to be the first on their block to have their own pet raccoon! Dogs and cats were once wild, too, it's true. But their domestication has occurred over millions of years. Animals that are wild today cannot be domesticated, not in our lifetime.

Wildlife experts are not crazy about wild animals in the classroom, and with good reason. For example, when children are taught to "rescue" animals who have fallen from their nest or are otherwise in danger, it can disorganize a very refined system. Most wild animal mothers can take very good care of their young without any help from us. And while we may see it as helping, many times we are doing nothing more than interfering with a natural process.

This point was beautifully illustrated to me when I was working on the third floor of an office building. There was a mourning dove nest and two sweet doves raising their young on the ledge just outside the window where I could watch their progress through the glass without upsetting them. I watched the birds build the nest and lay the eggs, and then, much to my delight, witnessed the hatching of the eggs and the raising of the young. I had become quite enamored of this lovely little family and looked forward to the day when the fledglings would fly from their nest, free and ready to meet the world. But on one particularly rainy day, I became alarmed as the water in the ledge rose and rose, finally submerging the nest and the little baby birds in the water. Frantic, I called the local wildlife hospital to ask if someone could come rescue the birds. The person on the other end of the line was *annoyingly* calm as she patiently explained to me that the parents were fully capable of protecting their young and that they would move the birds if they felt it was necessary. Devastated at the prospect of watching these babies drown, I returned to the window, helpless. Imagine my surprise when I found that the parents had indeed moved the birds to the uppermost sides of the rather tall nest, and that they were high and dry and waiting out the storm! Had the birds been removed from the nest there is no telling what trauma that would have caused the parents or how the babies would have eventually fared in the custody and care of humans.

Wild animals who are healthy have an amazing ability to survive and thrive. As humane educators, we need to share with children our wonder and amazement at the unique abilities wild animals have to make their way in this world. I am not so sure, however, that caging them and bringing them into a classroom gets that particular message across.

Dianne Sauve, executive director of Palm Beach County Animal Care and Control and former director of the Ocean Impact Foundation, a wildlife rehabilitation agency, has over ten years experience as a wildlife rehabilitator. She had plenty to say on the subject of wild animals in the classroom:

"Children can get mixed messages depending on the educator. If a humane educator has any animal—whether it's an eagle, an owl, any type of bird of prey or a mammal such as a opossum or raccoon—children can get very mixed messages, and it depends on how the handler goes about teaching the lesson. If the animal is held and cuddled and nuzzled and kissed, kids get the message that it's okay for some of us to have wild animals as pets. Many wild animals should never be kept and raised in captivity by anyone.

Wildlife rehabilitators who bring baby raccoons are especially doing a disservice, because kids should never attempt to raise a raccoon as a pet. Raccoons are high on the list as a rabies-vector species. They are an animal that can carry this virus and be asymptomatic. It's a hot virus, meaning that once you get it there is no cure for it. The other situation with raccoons is that once they reach puberty they become aggressive, whether they have been raised in captivity as a pet or not. The older they get, the more aggressive they get. Once the fun and the novelty wears off, people take them out and just release them, and they have no skills for survival after being raised in captivity.

"But if the educator is very professional the presence of an animal can serve another purpose in allowing young people to interact with these animals. This is especially true for socioeconomically disadvantaged kids, who may never get an opportunity to see and appreciate these types of animals up close. In doing so they may learn a respect that may otherwise never have been talked about in their family, their neighborhood or any other situations in these lower-income areas.

"Sometimes the public wants to help wild animals, and that should be encouraged, certainly. The key element that we continue to teach is that when an injured or supposedly orphaned wild animal is found people should call the experts and get help. People should be taught not to deal with the situation on their own, and children should not be allowed to talk their parents into keeping the animal, even for a few days. Twenty-four to forty-eight hours with a baby bird can mean life or death and metabolic bone disease if switched to the wrong diet, because some of these animals reach maturity in three to four weeks.

"For animals that people come across such as fledgling

birds, all of whom live on the ground for between three and five days before becoming fully fledged, these animals need to be left alone and nature has designed it this way. It is survival of the fittest. The parents are in the area and if they are left alone, they are on their own within about a week. If they are taken from the wild, brought to a facility, they usually regress and it is usually one to two months before they can be released back into the wild. Of course, we don't want to teach that all wild animals have the skills to make it without help when they are sick. All wild animals have the skills to make it by themselves when they are healthy, but typically what we have found is that the animals we see are there because of us. Many birds are there because of what we term 'species conflict'—for example, a bird may have been in a scuffle with a cat. Domestic cats don't belong outside. This is a situation we have created. Birds of prey that come in with signs of toxicity or organo-phosphate are sick because we use so much fertilizer and pesticides in our golf courses and farms.

"Having been the director of a wildlife hospital for ten years I would have to say that in the upper ninety percent of all the animals that have been brought to our doors, people have had a detrimental effect on wildlife either directly or indirectly. Most of the animals we get have been orphaned because their trees are cut down at the wrong time of the year. During nesting season, ospreys and certain owls end up with pesticide poisoning. Many ospreys, especially in Florida, will find their homes in trees on a golf course. Since they are predominantly fish eaters, they will catch the fish out of the pond on the golf course, which is fertilized constantly, which leads to this cycle: runoff in the water gets into the fish, the fish get into the osprey and we end up with organo-phosphates. The same holds true with many other species found in agricultural areas.

"Many of the screech owls that come into the center have been hit by a car. Their eyesight is excellent, especially at night, when they are chasing their prey, but they are not cognizant of the fact that there are people in cars. Many of our highways now pass through areas that are normal migration paths for wildlife. Out in the West, in the Rockies, so many of the open fields are fenced and cross-fenced, which has totally interrupted the migratory paths for mammals such as the elk and the bison and so forth. So you end up with animals who can't get to their normal feeding grounds because of fencing or highways. Even turtles and alligators who are on the move in the springtime seeking mates don't realize that the paths they have to cross have cars."

This is an important lesson for educators. We can share this information with our students and encourage them to take an interest in local issues that may affect wildlife—including campaigning and voting for animal-friendly candidates, writing letters to the editor about overuse of local lands, watching out for injured animals around construction sites, and more.

I have tried to present both sides of this controversy in the hope that educators will follow their own counsel and do what they believe is right in every situation. Many teachers will only invite you in if animals are included in the lesson so that their students may interact with them. Teachers rarely indicate that animals are not welcome. All the teachers and aftercare directors who call me do so because they have heard about the animals and how trustworthy they are. The purpose of humane education programs is to teach compassion for animals and encourage respect for all animals. If we are to do this, we must first be invited to come to a classroom. In order to do that, we must offer the teachers what *they* want. We can do that and still respect the animals if we keep in mind that as long as the animals are enjoying the attention, we are probably meeting the needs of all concerned.

6

Classroom Pets

"We enjoy a relationship with dogs and cats because the social boundaries do not exist. You don't have to be pleasant, polite, watch what you say, etc. You can do and say whatever you want with your pet and they still accept you."

—Dr. John Pitts, D.V.M.

Dr. John Pitts is a veterinarian and the author of *Animals in the Classroom*. He works for the Pet Care Trust Foundation, which funds a program to assist classroom teachers seeking to add "classroom pets" to their curriculum. Dr. Pitts has met with over 1,300 teachers in national workshops in order to help them understand the animals they would like to bring into their classrooms. He believes that there is a place for classroom pets in education, but only if the teacher is setting a good example by insuring that animal's health and well-being. This is a lesson in itself!

But there are more lessons to be learned through the interaction with classroom pets. Science and biology teachers, certainly, find having animals in the classroom to be a great help with teaching about animals and the science of keeping them alive and reproducing. But geography teachers can also use the animals as a focus when teaching about the places in the world where the animals originated and how they are acquired (which may or may not be a pleasant story). Art teachers can help students appreciate the beauty of an individual animal through an artist's eyes, and character education teachers can teach children about the six pillars of character through the care of a classroom pet that the children have come to know, respect and love.

I attended one of Dr. Pitt's workshops on classroom pets with much trepidation. I am not sure that I am completely on board with the idea of animals living out their lives in a classroom environment. I worry that kids who are disrespectful of animals may have occasion to harm them when the teacher is not present in the room, and that the noises in school, including shouting, fire drills, sirens and loudspeakers can be painful to sensitive ears. I think of the ferret in the movie "Kindergarten Cop" and the tiny cage he was kept in. (In the first place, ferrets are not the best choice for a classroom animal for small children. Their temperament and fragility make them a poor choice for clumsy and awkward handling.) During a fire drill, a child grabbed him out of his cage and, holding him in his hands, ran out of the building with him.

The potential for losing this little animal was very high, and it was clear that nobody had ever taught those kids about responsible ferret handling. Naturally, I have concerns about the weekend care of classroom pets, and their loneliness during spring, winter and summer breaks. And again, many animal advocates feel that keeping animals in classrooms (instead of their natural habitats or private homes), not for their own benefit or enjoyment, but for ours, is unethical. However, I decided to listen with an open mind, and I am glad I did. I learned something about differences of opinion and how keeping an open mind can lead to positive change.

Dr. Pitts opened his discussion with the visual image of animals languishing in classrooms across America. He shared with us that the thought of these animals and the substandard care they sometimes receive propelled him to launch a humane education project devoted to educating teachers on the proper selection, care and feeding of small animals. This mission was the impetus behind the Pet Care Trust Foundation's "Animals in the Classroom" workshops, which are held all over the country to help teachers understand that even small animals are sentient and are deserving of the care and attention usually showered upon household cats and dogs. He conducted a survey of teachers and found that twenty-eight percent of the respondents had an aquarium of some kind in their classroom with fish, twenty-six percent had small mammals, twenty-two percent had reptiles, twelve percent had invertebrates, and two percent had birds. But were they caring for these animals properly? Surely everyone could use a little guidance when it comes to keeping animals happy and healthy. During Dr. Pitts's full-day workshop, teachers learn about humane care of selected animals in their classrooms. They are all presented with a 100-page manual with suggested lesson plans for teaching science, math, animal behavior, nutrition, geography and art. "The primary lesson," insists Dr. Pitts, "is to help teachers and students understand how to care for animals in a compassionate and responsible manner, to foster respect and love for living creatures."

In *Animals in the Classroom*, Dr. Pitts cites Dr. A.G. Rudd and Dr. Alan Beck of Purdue University, who reveal in the article "Kids and Critters in Class Together" that "Twenty-five percent of teachers keep or invite animals into their classroom."[15] "If one quarter of American teachers keep animals," Dr. Pitts adds, "it is vital that teachers select suitable animals, teach animal responsibility, avoid risks and encourage compassion for life. Students learn from experience. Proper pet care bolsters responsibility, but negative experience only reinforces inhumane care of animals."

Dr. Pitts believes that teachers are not able to make this project truly their own without the aid of an experienced humane educator. "Teachers need good mentors to help support animal welfare, and they need local resources to sustain ongoing animal education. To help complement existing local humane education programs, I offer access to this workshop and resources, to assist shelters and humane societies in their ongoing efforts to educate children and adults in their communities."

Dr. Pitts recommends selecting small mammals, aquarium fish, birds, reptiles, amphibians and invertebrates as classroom pets, but not dogs, cats or wildlife. I was truly surprised to learn that Dr. Pitts advocates the incorporation of domestically raised rats as the number one animal for classroom observation. Rats make the best classroom pets, he says, because they are congenial, friendly and, when raised domestically, free of disease. Animal rights advocates will see the benefit of having schoolchildren bond with rats, because it will help them understand that laboratory testing on rats is inherently cruel. The American public winces at the sight of dogs, cats and primates in laboratories but accept that rats are used for cosmetic and other testing. Maybe if children see and handle a rat firsthand, they won't be so quick to dismiss their feelings and accept the abuse that they receive at the hands of vivisectors.

Aquarium fish, says Dr. Pitts, are another example of suitable classroom pets.[16] He advocates using good quality, new equipment with a high-quality heater that matches the size of the aquarium. "The biggest cause of death in fish is poor water quality," says Dr. Pitts. Making the water quality safe for fish is a lesson in ecology and science that the children will long remember. "Aquariums are a microcosm for the planet earth," teaches Dr. Pitts. "What we do to the water, we do to ourselves. This is a wonderful environmental lesson."

And while birds are not necessarily Dr. Pitts's number one recommendation for classroom pets, he acknowledges that members of the psittacine family (parrots, macaws and parakeets) are popular choices. Just asking a student to spell and define "psittacine" is an exercise in literacy, science, biology and comprehension. So he provides information on keeping parakeets happy and healthy as well. For example, teachers will learn that they should vary the perch size within the cages so that the birds do not suffer from constriction of their claws; that twist ties should never be used to secure fixtures to the cage bars because they contain lead; that eucalyptus perches are the best and that a mineral bar other than cuttlefish should be offered. Dr. Pitts advises against the inclusion of lovebirds, because they may be noisy and aggressive and not conducive to a classroom atmosphere.

The best part of the workshop for me was the discussion of leopard geckos. I am the proud guardian of two leopard geckos who were rescued by my son when someone he knew went to jail and left his geckos to fend for themselves. I read a book on the care and feeding of geckos, of course, but Dr. Pitt's lecture helped me to understand their needs and skills in so many ways that a book could not.

Geckos have been popular as pets for over twenty-five years and are very social animals. They need elevation and incandescent lighting or a full spectrum light so that they can metabolize their calcium. "I have my geckos on heat rocks!" I exclaimed proudly. But Dr. Pitts looked at me in horror and explained that if the "death rocks," as the professionals call them, malfunctioned, I would never know it and the geckos could get overheated (think "cooked"). He recommends a heating pad specially made for gecko tanks instead. He advocates enhancing the environment for your gecko with plants in pots such as ponytail palms or small cycads. "And don't forget to warn students that salmonella is a normal part of a reptile's flora," he cautions, "but it can make us very, very ill." And for teachers, geckos make great facilitators of conversations about Pakistan, the country where they originated.

Dr. David Brooks, Ph.D., agrees with Dr. Pitts that the idea of animals in the classroom has merit. This former principal and teacher is also the founder and director of the Center for Implementing Character Education and author of the books *The Case for Character Education* and *Implementing Character Education*. He related the following story to illustrate the impact animals in the classroom can have on students.

"I knew a teacher who was teaching a relatively unruly fifth grade in an elementary school. Well, this teacher had a puppy at home, a young golden retriever. One day she had to bring her puppy to school because she was going somewhere after school and it was necessary to bring the dog. The principal didn't know about this at all. The puppy came into the class and the kids actually started behaving better! And so she started to bring the puppy to school every day and the conduct in the class changed. When her principal found out that she had been bringing a dog to school, he said she would have to leave the dog at home. So the teacher invited the principal to come into the class and see for himself the difference, survey what the difference among the students was. So the principal came into the class and observed for himself that kids were caring for this dog. They were being empathetic; if the dog was whining they would pet the dog, and they were quiet so as not to scare the dog. . . . This was a very subtle way of teaching the character trait empathy. It was a wonderful experience.

"I have to say that any time I go into a classroom where teachers have animals, whether they be gerbils, rats, snakes, whatever, there is a different atmosphere in the classroom. I am very much an advocate of incorporating animals as a tool to help students learn to be compassionate and caring. There is all this evidence about the benefits of taking animals into senior centers and rest homes. There is a reason for that. Having animals come into the classroom is an opportunity to teach good character through all kinds of experiences. There is also an opportunity to short-circuit disruptive behaviors, such as mistreatment of animals. If there is an animal in the classroom, teachers will be able to observe how the individual students are treating that animal, which will open the opportunity to see if there is a kid being mean to an animal and if there are other indicators that we need to be looking at. So there is a real advantage to that kind of experience in the school."

In his capacity as a lecturer and facilitator of implementing character education into the schools, Dr. Brooks travels a great deal to help schools across the country find ways to make character count in their schools. One of the things he advocates is the inclusion of community resources and partnerships with entities such as the fire department. Did Dr. Brooks think there was room for the humane society among his list of prospective community partnerships? "Oh absolutely," said Dr. Brooks, "I really think that, just like the fire department, the humane society ought be coming into schools, not as entertainment like from the zoo or a wild animal park, but really bringing educational programs into the school to make kids aware that animals have feelings, that is the number one lesson, and that mistreating an animal is inappropriate and there are negative consequences to those actions.

"But they need to learn also that there are some real personal benefits to treating an animal with kindness and respect. . . . Animals give us unconditional love and I think that the humane society going in that direction can raise the level of awareness of the importance of animals in our lives. I talk about how advertising leaves impressions upon us in many ways. Language leads to attitudes and attitudes leads to behavior. If the language is that "we treat animals kindly," than the attitude will be that "we treat animals kindly," and the behavior will be treating animals kindly. And this can extend from the rabbit or the cat or the dog to a sister or a brother. I believe in humane education. I believe it should be a part of character education components and I believe that classroom animals play an important part in the development of those character traits we want to see in out citizenry."

Once teachers have their classroom pets in place, the best part of the lesson begins: the naming of a classroom pet. This really gets student's thinking and facilitates an amazing classroom discussion about the place of animals in our lives.

"Why should we name him at all?" asks Dr. Pitts. "I mean, we don't name our television set, our desk or our pencil. How is this different? Why does this animal need a name?" He advises teachers to ask this question and entertain the student's responses. Of course, the naming of animals individualizes them and makes them a part of the group or family. The name can be chosen through a contest, a group decision or any number of means, but the message is clear. Animals are individuals and should never be objectified.

And that is the epitome of humane education.

7

A Few Good Lesson Plans

"Teaching is not a lost art, but the regard for it is a lost tradition."

—Jacques Barzun

Lesson plans are easy and fun to create on your own, or you can find them ready to use in a variety of places. The *ASPCA Humane Education Resource Guide for Teachers*, available at www.aspca.org, and the *Humane Educator's Guidebook* (from the Association of Professional Humane Educators) both contain lesson plans that are excellent for humane educators and easy to incorporate for novice educators.

If you decide to create your own lessons, follow this

outline to insure that they will be thorough and sound:

1. Write out your goal, the purpose of your lesson: "To teach students about . . ." In Woody's Wisdom, below, for example, you will see that the goal is to teach students about responsibility to animals.

2. Write out the objective: "The students will be able to . . ." In Woody's Wisdom, the students will be able to list several items. . . .

3. List the materials needed to complete the lesson. Keep in mind any photocopies or transparencies, etc. In Woody's Wisdom the materials listed are the items contained within the suitcase.

4. List any preparatory activities.

5. Describe the activity length, e.g., "This lesson should take between 60 and 90 minutes."

6. Describe the procedure.

7. Add any additional information such as web links, vocabulary words, etc.

8. Point out tie-ins to standard curriculum, e.g., The lesson plan on zoonoses fits nicely with science and biology.

The following lesson plans are samples appropriate for different age groups. As you read through them, try to identify the goals and objectives of each. Teachers, especially, appreciate the thought that goes into developing a lesson plan using language that they use every day in their classroom preparation time.

Through Woody's Wisdom, based on the popular lesson that has become widely known as the Pet Suitcase, we can teach young children (including preschoolers) about the many responsibilities of companion-animal care. The lesson on zoonoses teaches students about the diseases that are universal to both human and non-human animals (such as the coryza virus—generally known as the common cold). And in Animals 101, we go over all the wonderful career opportunities available to students who want to carve out a career for themselves out of their love and respect for animals (that you have fostered)!

The Pet Suitcase was first taught to me by a creative and experienced teacher in Fort Lauderdale named Caroline Crane. Caroline works with the Broward County Humane Society and has been my mentor and friend throughout my adjustment from animal-facilitated therapist to humane educator. The Pet Suitcase is designed for children in pre-K through second grade, and its simplicity makes it easy for volunteers to jump right in and teach the lesson like an old pro. The colorful children's suitcase is filled with items a dog or cat would need for his or her day-to-day care, including an obedience school diploma, a stuffed toy cat (to represent companionship), treats and, in my program, an African-American Doctor Barbie, the veterinarian. (See the next page for a complete list.) The idea is for the children to take turns selecting an item from the suitcase so that we can discuss why Woody would need the item. Woody, for her part, sits very still and serious, taking it all in as I demonstrate the application of flea repellant, the use of a grooming brush and a toothbrush. A toothbrush! For Woody? Yes, there are new concepts to be learned. The kids all get stickers for their participation, and Woody gets teeny-tiny treats. It's all in good fun and the children learn that dogs and cats need lots of attention, supplies and care. For those children who live with animals, it brings a new awareness of what is involved in caring for a companion animal. For those who don't, it helps them appreciate why their parents might say no to a cat or dog. It could be the expense, the awesome commitment, or the obligations to an animal. In either case, they learn about animals and that's the whole point.

Woody's Wisdom

Lesson Plan Goal

To teach pre-K through second-grade students how to take care of dogs and cats so that they understand that living with a companion animal is a big responsibility.

Objectives

Children will be able to name three to five objects that dogs and cats need for their day-to-day care. Children will also be able to explain the role of these objects in the life of the dog or cat, e.g., dogs need flea combs to help control fleas, heartworm medicine to avoid heartworm infestation, and a dog bowl for their food, which they must be allowed to eat undisturbed.

Materials

Suitcase or tote bag, basket, or other suitable container, and pet care items:

Flea comb. Explain how fleas cause itching and also tapeworms.

Box of heartworm treatment such as Heartguard. Explain about heartworm disease in dogs and how it is caused by mosquitoes.

Dog brush. For grooming
Toothbrush and dog toothpaste. For good dental health
Dog bowl. D*on't ever bother a dog while he or she is eating.*
Collar. For the tag and lead
Leash or lead. Because of the leash law and to keep the dog safe
Tag and/or certificate. Explain what rabies is and why it is important that your dog or cat be current on his or her vaccinations.
Veterinarian (this can be a doll dressed as a vet, or you can take a picture you find on the Internet or in a magazine of someone dressed like a doctor). Talk about the reasons you might visit a vet.
Heart-shaped pillow or heart-shaped object of some kind (even cardboard or paper). To signify that an animal companion needs love
Stuffed cat or dog. To signify that animals need companionship when you are not home
Book about understanding pets. To facilitate understanding of the animal's needs
Dog toy. To reduce boredom and satisfy the animal's chewing needs
Cat toy. To reduce boredom in a house cat—this could lead to a discussion of why cats should be kept inside.
Small dog or cat bed or photo of a bed. Because dogs and cats need their own space.
Empty water bottle. Because dogs and cats need fresh water
Empty dog shampoo bottle. Because dogs need to be kept clean and flea-free

This lesson should take about an hour. Each child is asked to come to the suitcase and select an item and explain (as in show and tell) what each item may be used for. There are cute stickers available from the American Humane Association that are large and round with animal pictures and the text "I am a 'Be kind to animals' kid" that I give each child so that I know who has come up and selected an item.

Most dog/cat guardians have all or most of these items or can get them from their local vet, shelter or friends. For younger students, I usually pack a picture book to read after the suitcase game is over. *A Home for Nathan*, by Claudia Roll (available from the Snyder Foundation for Animals); *The Bookshop Dog*, by Cynthia Rylant; *Let's Get a Pup! Said Kate*, by Bob Graham; and *How Smudge Came*, by Nan Gregory, are some of my favorite books to include with this lesson. There are so many others that can be found online or through national organizations such as American Humane Association or Humane Society of the United States. Be selective, however, in the books you choose to read to children, because not all so-called animal books have a pro-animal message. Be sure there is no animal cruelty, no matter how minor. Look for books that discuss individual animals' needs, advocate respect for nature and show compassion for animals and people alike.

The books listed above also provide the benefit of showing cultural differences. In *A Home for Nathan*, Nathan the cat, after visiting an African-American veterinarian, comes home to a family comprised of two women as well as other household pets. In *The Bookshop Dog*, the Caucasian store owner marries a person of color. In *Let's Get a Pup! Said Kate*, the parents have body piercings and tattoos. And *How Smudge Came* is a story of a puppy rescued by a person with Down Syndrome. I love that these books show diversity, because the children sitting in the classrooms are from a wide variety of families and cultural backgrounds. These are stories that everyone can relate to. I am certain there are many more such books available, and the search for them is half the fun!

If you really want to impress the teacher, look up the state standards in your state's educational system for each subject. This is a mandated level of proficiency in each subject, differing from state to state, that students must demonstrate before graduating to the next grade level. Teachers must give a specific number of hours of instruction in math, writing, comprehension, etc. Use lessons that incorporate these subjects and you help the teachers meet their quota for hours spent on each subject. The following lesson plan for elementary school students adheres to state standards for information management, effective communication and critical and creative thinking.

Zoonoses and You

Overview/Objective

This lesson shows that animals can share many of the same diseases with human animals. The students will be able to discuss the difference between a mammal and a non-mammal and which of these are subject to rabies and other zoonotic diseases.

Materials

Microscope
Slides
Specimens
Photos of parasites
Vocabulary list
Power point or overhead photos of specimens (available through your local vet)

Preparation

- Prepare slides with ticks, fleas, worms, etc. Your local humane society or your own veterinarian can furnish these items to you. They may allow you to use an extra microscope; otherwise, ask the teacher if there is one in the science department you may use.
- Prepare overhead transparencies or Power Point slides with photos of an assortment of animals. Include mammals, reptiles, birds, fish and rodents.

Activity Length

One to two hours depending on class size and interactions.

Procedures

- Tell the students that many of the same diseases that animals get can be shared with humans. Ask if any student can name any of the diseases. Write their answers on the board.
- Hand out the vocabulary list and go through the words.
- Show your transparencies or Power Point slides. As you point to each photo, ask the students to tell you if this animal can get rabies or not, and why or why not. For very young students you can use puppets and have the puppets ask the question, "Can I get rabies? Why or why not?"
- Have the students take turns viewing the slides under the microscope and discussing what they see there.

Web Links

http://animalpetdoctor.homestead.com/Zoonotics.html
www.vetinfo.com

Cyber Hunt

Give each child a keyword and ask them to search on the

Internet, using the links provided or a search engine such as "Yahoo," "DogPile" or "Ask Jeeves," to see what they can find, then bring the results back to a subsequent class. Keywords include rabies, parasites, worms, flatworms, roundworms, tapeworms, fleas, ticks, mad rabies, dumb rabies, zoonotics.

For the older students, our presentation focuses on the interpretation of canine and feline body language and avoiding dog and cat bites. The Dogz in the Hood program is based on Caroline Crane's animal communication lessons and involves overhead transparencies, and, of course, live animal demonstrations as Woody and Katie stand patiently while child after child asks the important questions "May I pet your dog?" and "Is she friendly?" And even though my partners know full well that they are to stand quietly and seriously while this exercise continues, they can't help but to show their unmitigated joy at being part of all the fun!

Dogz in the Hood

Overview

This lesson is intended to teach children how to recognize and identify some aspects of a dog's body language.

Goal

To teach students how to avoid dog bites

Objective

Students will be able to identify three aspects of a dog's body language that indicate his or her mood and possible action.

Activity length

1 hour

Materials

Using overhead transparencies or slides, show images of dogs in various positions that demonstrate their body language. (You can make photos into slides or transparencies by assorted humane education materials from organizations such as the Anti-Cruelty Society of Chicago. Another source is dog behavior books, though you must always obtain permission from the publisher if you want to reproduce a photograph from a book. Many of the guidebooks and lesson plan books described elsewhere in this book will have pictures of dogs in a variety of poses that indicate what they are about to do.)

Presentation

If you have an assistance dog, demonstrate on the dog how a tail can be shown flagging or wagging (wagging is entire tail and is a sign of joy and friendship; flagging is just the tip of the tail held straight up and indicates fear or aggression); show where the hackles are (the area of fur between the dog's shoulder blades that will stand on end when a dog is aroused) and the positioning of the ears (if they are flat or forced forward, that is a sign the dog is feeling fear or aggression.)

Explain to the students that if they see a dog who is showing signs of aggression they should never run; rather, they should try shouting at the dog in a commanding voice "NO!" or offer the dog something to bite, such as a book bag or book, and place something between themselves and the dog, such as a bicycle. If they are under attack, they should curl in a ball and protect their front where the most vital organs are and try to fend off the dog using whatever is handy.

The above lesson can also be offered for postal workers, delivery drivers and others who come into contact with strange dogs.

Our intention is not to scare children into believing that all dogs are vicious, only to give them the tools to recognize when a dog may bite or attack. There are a number of excellent videos available from the Latham Foundation and even State Farm insurance that demonstrate how to react to dog bites.

You may find in the course of teaching humane education that there are a number of students who want to explore the idea of careers in working with animals. For them, we have included a lesson suitable for middle school kids who may be thinking about a career in service to animals.

Animals 101

Overview

This lesson is intended to help children who are thinking of going into a career involving animals and animal care. The children will be asked at the beginning of the class to share their animal-career goals.

Objective

To teach students how early involvement in humane societies and rescue groups will be an asset in their stated career goals; and how using their natural curiosity talents for writing, art, web mastering, public speaking and drama can help them reach their goals.

Goals

Students will understand and be able to define animal advocacy and the difference between animal rights, animal welfare and animal control. Students will understand and be able to cite three laws that exist to protect animals against cruelty and neglect. Students will be able to state three reasons why responsible animal care is important and will be able to discuss costs associated with caring for an animal, and the importance of spay/neuter and early training techniques. Students will understand how a law is made, using an animal law as a model. This lesson builds character and encourages good citizenship.

Activity Length

One to two hours, depending on questions and discussion

Preparation

The teacher may ask the students to list animal careers prior to the presentation and then check them off as they are mentioned. The book *Careers in Helping Animals* and/or other books on careers in animal care should be readily available. As the students list possible careers, have them discuss what educational requirements are needed for each one. Check your book to make sure that the information is valid. Include such careers as the following:

Animal Careers

- Animal artist
- Animal behaviorist
- Animal control officer
- Animal trainer (e.g., dog obedience training)
- Animal writer/researcher/author
- Applied behavior psychologist
- Humane officer
- Pet supply store associate
- Police officer specializing in animal crimes
- Primatologist
- Veterinarian
- Veterinary technician
- Wildlife artist
- Wildlife photographer
- Zoologist

Volunteer Opportunities

- Animal-assisted therapy
- Animal hospitals
- Animal shelters
- Canine Companion Puppy Foster Parent
- Crafts
- Foster care for orphaned or ill animals
- Letter-writing to help with animal legislation
- Wild animal sanctuaries
- Writing/photographing/drawing/web mastering for animal charity

Responsibility in Companion Animal Care

- Spaying and neutering health benefits
- Spaying and neutering as a means of controlling population
- Veterinary care including vaccines, dental health, heartworm prevention, flea prevention and the importance of keeping cats indoors and dogs on leads
- Getting involved in helping stray animals
- How to respond to emergencies involving animals
- How to handle cruelty matters, when to call the police, how to report abuse
- Helping animals through legislative action: how you vote; helping to facilitate laws

Other Careers That Can Help Animals

- Art: Selling animal-themed artwork and donating money to animal causes
- Journalist: Expose writing and reporting
- Miscellaneous: Accounting, secretarial, emergency driver
- Photography: Facilitating respect for animals
- Public health nurses and doctors
- Web mastering: Working for an animal organization

•Writing books and magazine articles about animals

Be friendly and encouraging. Don't invalidate any ideas; try to think of ways the student's ideas can fit in with animal careers, and invite students to visit the local shelter or clinic. Be sensitive to differing cultures and try to persuade through friendly give and take. Do not be "preachy."

Here is a list of vocabulary terms commonly used by those in professions that involve animals. You may copy and distribute or copy this onto an overhead transparency and go over the words as a class. Or you may put definitions and words on separate pages and have the students match the definitions with the terms.

Commonly used veterinary terms

ADR (ain't doing right). Commonly used veterinary term for when an animal is not exhibiting any distinct signs or symptoms of illness but is not doing well overall

Alpha dog. A dog that wants to be in charge; the dominant dog of a group

Animal husbandry. A branch of agriculture concerned with the production and care of domestic animals

Backyard breeder. Someone who breeds a lot of dogs and whose primary motivation is money, not the love of the breed. They pay little attention to the health of the animals in their care.

Behavior modification. The process of learning to substitute desirable responses and behavior patterns for undesirable ones

Bitch. A female dog

Blaze. The patch of white on an animal's chest

Breed conformation. A specific look that all purebred dogs or cats have. For example, all Great Pyrenees dogs must be white and have thick fur.

Breed standard. The traits an animal must exhibit to be considered a particular breed. For example, the breed standard for poodles is that they have floppy ears and curly coat.

Dam. The female parent of an animal

Euthanasia. Literally "good death"; the act of putting an animal to death humanely

Fear-biter. A usually calm animal that will bite when fearful

Fix. A slang word meaning to spay or neuter

Gentle Leader. A specialized type of collar that goes on the dog's snout instead of the neck

Heel. A command that tells an animal to walk neatly by your side

Litter. A group of puppies or kittens born at the same time to the same mother

Neuter. To remove the testicles of a male animal so that he cannot reproduce

Pedigree. An ancestral line; an animal's origin and history

Purebred. Bred from members of a recognized breed, strain, or kind without cross-breeding over many generations

Queen. A mother cat

Resource guarding. Occurs when dogs are especially protective of their food and/or toys. May cause biting.

Responsible breeder. A person who is very careful about passing on genetic traits in animals and who helps with rescue of specific breeds

Separation anxiety. A disorder whereby the dog is afraid of being alone.

She-cat. A female cat.

Sire. The male parent of an animal, especially a domestic animal
Spay. To remove the ovaries of a female animal so that she cannot reproduce
Sterilize. A word generally used for spaying and/or neutering
Tom. An unneutered male cat
Whelp. To give birth to a litter of puppies or kittens
Withers. The ridge between the shoulder bones of a dog or cat, commonly used to measure the animal's height (e.g., fifteen inches from floor to withers)
Zoonosis. Disease that can be communicated to both human and non-human animals

Here are some words we use to describe cat colors. Explain that knowing the different colors for cats is important because if you report your Tortie missing and describe her as black and brown, you may not get your cat back!

Calico. Multicolored patches on a predominantly white coat
DLH. Domestic Long Hair
DSH. Domestic Short Hair
Ginger. Orange
Persian. One of several breeds of cat with long hair
Siamese. Distinct markings about the face, ears, paws and tail
Tabby. Silver or brown undercoat with large black stripes in an asymmetrical pattern. When a bullseye is formed, the cat is called a bullseye tabby.
Tiger. Silver or brown undercoat with large black stripes in a symmetrical pattern
Tortoiseshell. Shades of brown, red, gold and black

blended together. Also called "tortie."

Here are some fun words that you can use to make a match game. Write the animals on the board, then read the words that describe a quantity and see who can pick the right ones (make it fun, make silly comments along the way!).

- A **herd** of antelopes
- A **flock** of birds
- A **brood** of chickens
- A **murder** of crows (*Wow, where did that one come from?*)
- A **clutch** of eggs
- A **gang** of elk *(Animals in gangs! Must not have enough love at home!)*
- A **school** of fish *(See, you are not the only ones!)*
- A **gaggle** of geese
- A **troop** of kangaroos *(Hope they don't send them to war!)*
- An **exaltation** of larks—this one is SURE to stump them!
- A **leap** of leopards (*Leaping leopards? Who came up with that one? Who writes this stuff?*)
- A **pride** of lions *(They SHOULD be proud!)*
- A **troop** of monkeys
- A **litter** of puppies, kittens or mice
- A **covey** of quail
- A **bevy** of swans
- A **pod** of whales, dolphins or seals
- A **pack** of wolves (*What else comes in a pack? Dogs!*)

These lists are not complete, but the idea is to teach children that many professions have unique languages and that those working with animals have a language all their own as well. There is a complete vocabulary list in the appendix that you may copy and distribute. Be sure to do so before every lesson so that the students can look up any words they may not be familiar with. You may want to make a game of it and have them check off the vocabulary words as you use them and then offer a prize for the student that has the most words checked off.

The next lesson plan is ideal for high school students. It incorporates math and social studies and teaches about the link between overpopulation of unwanted animals and euthanasia.

It's Raining Cats and Dogs

Use statistical data to solve a real-life community problem.

Overview

This interactive lesson focuses on a community problem by measuring the annual adoption rate of sterilized animals to determine if sterilization before adoption reduces the euthanasia rate.

Preparation

- Gather materials for activity/presentation
- Call humane education department of humane society to schedule a presentation.
- Make copies of surveys and contact information. For your county's specific statistics, call your local animal control agency.

Materials

- Contact names, e-mail addresses and numbers for several area animal shelters that offer animals for adoption and perform spay/neuter and euthanasia
- Survey Recording sheet for estimates and measurements
- Pencils
- 200-300 buttons, craft sticks, pom-poms, Skittles, or other small candy or item

Activity Length

Approximately one hour. The homework component can take five to seven days.

Procedures

Definitions

Write the following words on the board (or include the list in a Power Point presentation) and ask the students to tell you what they mean: The accompanying definitions are a guide; the students should come very close to these definitions.

- **Euthanasia.** The humane killing of unwanted animals
- **Humane Society.** An organization to help stray, abandoned or unwanted animals
- **Heat.** The period during a female cat or dog's hormone cycle during which she can become pregnant
- **Intact.** An animal that has not been spayed or neutered
- **Neuter.** A surgical procedure to remove a male animals' ability to contribute to the creation of baby animals
- **Overpopulation.** Too many animals and not enough homes for them all
- **Spay.** A surgical procedure to remove a female animal's ability to have babies
- **Sterilization.** A gender-neutral word to describe both spaying and neutering

Guided Discussion

Ask students if they have dogs or cats at home.

1. Of the students who raise their hands, ask if they know if their animals are spayed or neutered before allowing them to answer the question. Do not react if they are not, but

congratulate them if they are.

2. Discuss the problems a community encounters when there are too many animals and not enough homes. Tell them that some national statistics put the annual number of euthanasias performed nationally as high as 15 million. Ask the students how they feel about spaying and neutering in general.
3. Ask the students how *they feel* about euthanasia.
4. Play a game of give-away. Give each student a photo of a cat or dog, or you can use an object such as a button or pom pom. Tell the student that each item represents a cat (or dog). Take a pom pom from one child and give it to another, then give it back to the original student and say:

   "Your cat (or dog) went *to visit* (roll your eyes or otherwise indicate that this is a metaphor) his/her cat, and 63 days later she gave birth to kittens (or puppies)."

   Give the student 6 or 8 more pom poms. Continue this randomly around the room until almost everyone has a handful of pom poms.

   Ask the students to ask several others in the room if they want a puppy/kitten. Tell the students that the student with only one or two dogs/cats is the "winner" and the goal is to reduce number of dogs/cats. Nobody will want to take on other dogs/cats, except for the few students whose dogs/cats didn't "go visit" another student's dog/cat.

   Ask the students to discuss ways in which the number of unwanted kittens (or puppies) can be reduced.

Answers *may* include

- Education regarding pet stores and their connection to puppy mills
- Behavior modification
- Breeding ban ordinance
- Fine on breeders
- Spaying and neutering mandates
- Breeding moratorium

Hand out the information sheets with the contact information for several area shelters and ask the students to contact the shelters and ask the questions on the survey below. This can be done either as an individual project or a team project.

Homework component: Give the students a set amount of time to have the survey completed. Ask them to come up with a solution to the overpopulation problem and then write a persuasive argument (100-150) word essay.

During the interim, you may want to schedule a presentation by calling your local humane society and asking for a speaker.

After the surveys are completed, ask the students to chart or graph the results to show how the number of euthanasias in shelters that only adopt sterilized animals compares with the number of euthanasias performed in shelters that adopt animals who are released intact.

Have the students discuss their findings. This

could also be a topic for a debate within the class or debate team project.

As a followup, students may want to write to their local legislators to ask for laws requiring that all animals adopted from a shelter be sterilized.

The use of a Power Point presentation, with colorful slides, special effects such as cool noises and transitions and kids love technology.

Cyber hunt
Give each child a keyword and ask them to search on the Internet, using the links provided or a search engine such as "Yahoo," "DogPile" or "Ask Jeeves," to see what they can find and bring the results back to a subsequent class. Keywords include spay, neuter, companion animals, euthanasia, overpopulation, humane society, breeding.

Web links
The Humane Society of the United States
www.hsus.org/programs/companion/overpopulation/petowner_stats.html

Extensions/Modifications (How can this lesson be modified for specific learners?)

- For ESOL students, HSUS (contact information above) has literature and posters available in Spanish.
- ESE students can role-play by taking on the role of the director of a local shelter and solve the problem of pet overpopulation.

The lesson can be extended by having the students multiply the number of animals one cat (or dog) can have in their lifetime if not sterilized. For example: One female cat that lives ten years is capable of going into heat four times per year and having eight kittens per litter. How many kittens will that cat have in her lifetime? How many kittens will that cat and all her female kittens have in a lifetime?

Sample Survey Questions

- How long has your shelter been in existence?
- How many employees does your shelter have?
- How many veterinarians does your shelter have?
- What is the number of sterilizations performed on shelter animals every day?
- What is the number of sterilizations performed on non-shelter animals everyday?
- How many dogs do you adopt out each week?
- How many cats do you adopt out each week?
- How many puppies (under six months) do you adopt out each week?
- How many kittens (under six months) do you adopt out each week?
- Does your shelter euthanize surplus animals?
- If so, how many animals were euthanized in the last calendar year?
- How many animals were euthanized in the year previous to the last calendar year?
- If you do not euthanize, do you send animals to another facility to be euthanized?
- If so, how many did you send to another facility in the last calendar year?
- And the year before that?
- Do you sterilize all animals prior to adoption?
- If not, do you require a deposit to be returned when the animal is sterilized?

- Try to determine from the answers above which shelters have a lowered euthanasia rate due to sterilization prior to adoption.

Find your own style when writing and implementing lesson plans; this will be the hallmark of your program. The resources in this chapter and in the appendix will help you get off to a great start. Remember to keep it fun and friendly, and you will do just fine.

8

Animal-Assisted Activity and Animal-Assisted Therapy

A child's life is like a piece of paper on which every person leaves a mark.

—Chinese proverb

Some humane education presentations are very formal, with goals and objectives, lesson plans and prescribed outcomes; but others are informal gatherings where the educator takes a back seat to the animals and lets the conversation ebb and flow with the moment. These are the times when children bare their very souls and social service workers are treated to epiphanies and breakthroughs. In these situations, are humane educators actually providing what is known as animal-assisted therapy?

According to studies published by Purdue University, the inclusion of companion animals in a child's life enhances the child physiologically and socially and heightens his or her capacity to learn. This is hardly surprising, when the benefits of human-animal interaction have been so well established in another population: the elderly. Clinical reports of interactions with animals and the aged number in the hundreds. They consistently show that when animals are involved in the lives of the elderly, or those afflicted with Alzheimer's disease, arteriosclerosis, depression or a reduction of energy and zest for life, the patients smile more, laugh more and become more socially communicative. They cooperate with their caregivers more freely and are just more pleasant to be around. Some studies, concentrating on residents of nursing homes or care centers, reveal that the petting, talking and interaction with an animal serves as a catalyst for communication for residents too depressed or lethargic to intermingle with other residents. Animals in these settings also provide occasion for physical therapy as the residents bend and stretch to stroke a gentle dog, or lift a purring cat.

The Delta Society has outlined the terminology used in activities that involve animals. According to the Delta Society, animal-assisted activities (AAA) and animal-assisted therapy (AAT) are the preferred terms; other terms that are used are "pet-facilitated therapy" and "animal-facilitated therapy," but "pet therapy" should be avoided because it is an archaic term that referred to behavior training programs for animals. The preferred terms (AAA and AAT) imply that the animal is the motivating force that enhances treatment provided by a certified, registered or otherwise well-trained person.

The definition of animal-assisted activity, as provided by the Delta Society, is: "AAA provides opportunities for motivational, educational, recreational, and/or therapeutic benefits to enhance quality of life. AAA are delivered in a variety of environments by specially trained professionals, paraprofessionals, and/or volunteers, in association with animals that meet specific criteria."[17]

What this means is that AAA is the term we use when we talk about informal activities that incorporate animals in which the animals are the primary focus of the activity. When Woody and Katie come to visit classrooms or groups of children and they are the focus of the lesson, this would be an example of animal-assisted activity. When we demonstrate with a live dog the safe way to greet a dog, avoid dog bites by reading body language or exhibit proper canine dental care or brushing of a dog's coat, this would be considered animal-assisted activity. Unlike animal-assisted therapy, there are no "treatment goals" related to a specific illness, there is no requirement to take detailed notes and the visits can last as long as the animal, the handler and the kids are comfortable and involved. Taking a dog or cat to a nursing home, visiting with school kids to discuss animal-related issues and giving demonstrations of basic obedience at scout meetings or other gatherings are all examples of animal-assisted activities.

Animal-assisted therapy differs from animal-assisted activity in that the incorporation of an animal is prescribed as part of a treatment process with a therapeutic intervention and special, prearranged criteria. The formal definition of animal-assisted therapy is:

"AAT is a goal-directed intervention in which an animal that meets specific criteria is an integral part of the treatment process. AAT is directed and/or delivered by a health/human service professional with specialized expertise, and within the scope of practice of his/her profession.

"AAT is designed to promote improvement in human physical, social, emotional, and/or cognitive functioning. AAT is provided in a variety of settings and may be group or individual in nature. This process is documented and evaluated."[18]

Those who are involved with animal-assisted therapy are usually seeing patients and must keep detailed records of the visit to share with a physician or therapist. Some examples of animal-assisted therapy are:

- An occupational therapist is assisted by a dog and his or her handler in work to increase a person's range of motion in the shoulder. The person has the specific goal of increasing her ability to reach toward one of her feet. The dog knows specialized commands that are used during the sessions. The progress made during each session is documented by the occupational therapist.

- A mental health professional incorporates a guinea pig in working with a small group of adults with developmental disabilities. People in the group are working on improving their communication and social skills. The professional documents the results of each session in each person's chart.[19]

At Mount Sinai Hospital in New York City, dogs have been incorporated into rehabilitation programs for victims of brain and spinal-cord injuries. In Richmond, Virginia, there is a Lhasa apso who specializes in relaxing shock-therapy patients, and in Texas, dogs help motivate children recovering in burn units and calm Alzheimer's patients. These are some examples of ways in which formal animal-assisted therapy is used.

While humane education does not normally qualify as animal-assisted therapy, humane education presentations can undoubtedly have therapeutic value. When a therapist asks a child, "How does that make you feel?" he or she may very well be met with quiet resistance. However, when Katie rolls over on her back and a child becomes lost and absorbed in her luxuriant coat, the "grown ups" in the room dissolve and the child begins to share things with Katie that he or she would never say out loud to someone who is efficiently taking notes and nodding in understanding. These moments are both therapeutic and educational, precious and few.

There is a social work program in our school system that reaches out to children who have very little, if any, social graces. The program is called "social skills" class. The students who are invited to come to the social skills class are those who have had some difficulties in school that cause school officials to suspect that there is some kind of abuse taking place in the home or extended family. The social workers who manage and facilitate these classes bring the group together for after-school meetings and try to determine what is going on at home and how the kids can be helped. The students range in age from eight to eleven, and there may typically be anywhere from ten to fifteen kids in any given group.

In a scenario like this, there is little chance that a formal humane-education program will be very successful. These are kids who barely have the wherewithal to care for themselves, let alone a companion animal. But the presence of a gentle dog can and does bring about some vital revelations that the social worker may then expand upon.

In one such group, there was Ellie, a young African-American girl who had a severe weight problem. It was certain that her self-esteem suffered, as she was the butt of many cruel jokes and comments during the day. The circumstances of her home life were virtually unknown to the social worker, because Ellie rarely spoke. When she did, her words were usually harsh and full of anger. Woody and Katie and I were invited to accompany the social worker while she facilitated the group one day after school. We met in the media center, and the dogs and I were seated comfortably on the floor when the bell rang. Within a few minutes, kids started trickling into the media center. One by one, they came over and asked about the dogs—"Those your dogs? Can I pet him? Do they bite? Can I touch him? Can I walk him?" I answered their questions, explaining that Woody and Katie were girl dogs and that they had come to visit with the group today at the request of Ms. Becky, the school social worker.

When Ellie entered the room she barely glanced at the dogs. She sat on a chair facing the table, away from the group, and put her head on the table. Ms. Becky asked her to join us, but Ellie refused. So for a while the little group sat in a circle discussing the dogs, what they ate, where they lived and so on. Ellie watched us out of the corner of her eye but didn't make any attempt to become part of the group.

Finally, Katie decided that the group needed to be together. Maybe it was her Australian Shepherd's herding instinct that caused her to saunter over to Ellie and place her head on Ellie's lap. "She wants you to join us," I said. Ellie didn't answer, but she placed a pudgy finger on Katie's head, just between her ears, and stroked her uncertainly. Katie's response, as it always is, was to drop to the ground and roll over on her back, begging for a belly rub. Ellie slipped off her chair and was soon lost in the luxury of Katie's beautiful, long coat. Ms. Becky and I glanced at one another hopefully. Could this lead to something? Could we possibly have a breakthrough imminent?

"I see you like dogs, huh?" I began, hopefully. The rest of the group was still circled around Woody, who was delighted at this new development. She had the kids to herself for a change, not sharing the spotlight with Katie! Ellie nodded silently. "Do you have a dog?" I asked. "I did once," Ellie whispered, not looking at us but staring into Katie's fur. "What happened to him?" I asked. "My mom done run him off. She said she didn't like him no more and that he was dirty and noisy and she chased him away with a broomstick." "I'm sorry," I said. "I guess you must miss him." Ellie simply nodded. Ms. Becky asked Ellie if she ever told her mom how she felt, that she missed her dog. Ellie didn't answer. Katie looked up at Ellie and gave her a kiss, and Ellie giggled. Becky whispered that it was one of the "very few times" she had ever seen Ellie smile. It was such a treat to see her smile, if even for a moment. Becky tried again "You know, if you told your mom how much you miss your dog, maybe she will let you have another one." I shot her a look—the last thing I wanted was to allow Ellie's mom the opportunity to abandon another poor dog! But it was simply strategy on Becky's part, and it seemed to work. "Naw," said Ellie, "She just tell me to shut up. She just tell me that I could run away too and she wouldn't care. She just hit me with the broomstick."

Of course, an hour's visit with two nice dogs cannot possibly fix this little girl's life, and I am not suggesting that it can. But Ellie's disclosure gave her teacher some insight as to what might be going on in Ellie's home and in her mind.

It gave her a starting point from which to launch an all-out effort to help this little one. And that's a big enough job for a dog!

The knowledge that we may have helped in some significant way, however small, to bring about a little health and happiness in Ellie's life is priceless and rewarding. These opportunities present themselves at every turn, and when they do it is such an honor to be a part of it.

In her book, *Why the Wild Things Are*,[20] Gail F. Melson writes that "Animals tend to bring out the best not only in children with disabilities, but in the people who interact with them." She explains that "A major problem for children with disabilities of various kinds—physical, emotional, mental—is that other children and adults often avoid them. Even in the 'inclusive' classrooms where children with disabilities are 'mainstreamed' with typically developing children, inclusion is usually only name-deep. When free play comes, the children without disabilities congregate together, segregating themselves and excluding those with handicaps. At the grocery store, in the mall, on the playground, eyes are studiously averted. A spastic child with uncontrollable, jerky movements and a twisted expression is not a conventionally 'pleasant' sight. Negative attitudes toward people with disabilities show up in children as young as age five."[21] Melson goes on to describe how the presence of service dogs enhances the lives of these children. "Something remarkable happens when a service dog . . . accompanies a wheelchair-bound child," she writes. "In one study researchers trailed three girls and two boys, each between ten and fifteen years old, in a wheelchair and using a trained service dog. As the youngsters navigated their wheelchairs and their dogs though school corridors and shopping mall lanes, the researchers recorded the 'social acknowledgments,' the friendly glances, smiles and conversations that schoolmates and passersby at the mall directed at the children." They then followed wheelchair-bound kids without dogs, who did not get any recognition. The results of this survey prove that the presence of service dogs brought an element to the children's lives that was not available to the kids without service dogs.

This may help to explain why an extraordinary program that incorporates reading aloud to dogs and has been helping kids all over the country is such a hit. Some kids have trouble reading aloud in front of their classmates. If they have accents or read with hesitation or haltingly, they are perceived as "different" or maybe "slow." But each week Woody and Katie visit the children's section of the city library so they can listen to children read stories. The children who read to them are learning to be more open to reading aloud and in doing so are becoming better readers.

Nancy Coriarity, children's librarian at the West Palm Beach City Library, is enthusiastic about the program. "The dogs never complain or criticize when the kids make a mistake while reading; they just listen quietly. The kids are lining up to read to the dogs. Did you ever think you would see kids lining up for the opportunity to read out loud? Some kids even whine until their turn. It is absolutely amazing." Children who are speakers of languages other than English are especially shy about reading out loud in front of their classmates, but Woody and Katie make it easy to read out loud, because English is not their first language either! In this way, again, we are helping to build self-esteem and confidence. Naturally, the books we choose are all animal-friendly with animal-advocacy themes. We never miss a beat!

Kay Heisler is a character education teacher with whom I

work on a regular basis. She is a delight to be with and a clever and sagacious educator. There is a little song that Kay has her class sing to the dogs whenever we come to visit. The song is "I Think You're Wonderful"[22] and the lyrics are:

I think you're wonderful
When somebody says that to me
I feel wonderful
As wonderful can be
It makes me want to say
The same thing to somebody new
And by the way I've been meaning to say
I think you're wonderful too

When we practice this phrase in the most honest way
Find something special in someone each day
You lift up the world one heart at a time
It all starts by saying this one simple line

(Chorus)

When each one of us feels important inside
Loving and giving and glad we're alive
Oh what a difference we're making each day
And all because someone decided to say

(Chorus)

The words that Kay has her class sing to the dogs teaches the kids that animals, as well as humans, need that validation, that pat on the back, that feel-good motivation that keeps us all going. And while having kids sing songs to dogs is not per se a humane education lesson, there is a valuable lesson being learned. "It is important that the children see us interacting with the dogs you bring," says Kay. "Allowing them to sing to the dogs and watching us respect their needs is a powerful lesson in itself."

We know how dogs can enhance the lives of school children, patients in hospitals and rehabilitation centers, but they also can be called in at a moment's notice to help out in times of great stress, as happened early in 2003 during a tragic nightclub fire in Rhode Island that took the lives of ninety-six people. Says Jane Deming, Director of Humane Education for the Providence Animal Rescue League, "A couple of days after the fire I got a phone call from a friend of mine who is the director of the northeast chapter of a search dog organization. He said there were three to four hundred family members and victims waiting in a special hotel room to find out whether their family members had survived or died. They were still looking for people; they had burn victims that they could not identify. So many were burned beyond recognition, and many of the burn victims in hospitals weren't yet identified because their clothes were burned completely off and all their belongings.

"So these four hundred or so family members are waiting in this big hotel room that emergency management set up with the governor and clergy members, and what they were trying to do was bolster these people up as the news came in about their loved ones. There was a couple whose twenty-three-year-old son had died in the fire. He was all they had in the whole world, their only living relative. They got the news that his body had been found. But the process of identifying the bodies was long and tortuous; it was days and days going through the building and trying to find them and even trying to find more victims. And he called me and said, 'I need some therapy dogs.' American Red Cross had called him and asked who we knew in Rhode Island with therapy dogs."

The dogs don't know if the person they are visiting and to whom they are ministering is bereaved, troubled or imprisoned. They do their job without judgment, without pity and without question. They can be especially helpful with kids who come from dysfunctional families. Psychotherapist Peggy McKeal had this to say about dysfunctional families and how the inclusion of animals in their therapy, however informal, lends itself to change: "Children can pick up very quickly if they think somebody's okay or not. This is especially true of children who come from very dysfunctional homes. They pick it up like that because they are visual and they hear. They put it all together. So if you are effusive with a child but you are not genuine they know that. Animals are genuine. They are not judgmental, they are not phony, they are not going to report you and there are not negative consequences in telling an animal your secrets. Using animals as therapists works because it gives the child something to focus on, something to look at and talk to besides the human who is fastidiously taking notes."

This is the secret behind the success of the program at the world-famous Best Friends Animal Sanctuary. Nathania Gartman was one of the founders of this unique facility in a little town called Kanab, nestled in Angel Canyon in the red mountains of Utah. Nathania was a humane educator living and working at the sanctuary. Before succumbing to cancer in July, 2003, she told me a bit about her program. "Our program at Best Friends is somewhat different from other animal-assisted therapy programs," she told me. "We have a lot of young people from therapeutic programs or court-ordered programs. We have a lot of kids who come from private schools who are often at risk for other reasons. Some of those kids are at risk because of emotional distance from their families. We have expanded the concept of what an 'at-risk' kid is to make it larger. We have kids who come to us at fifteen or sixteen years old who don't know how to sweep or clean or do anything because they come from such wealthy families that everything is done for them. And there are kids who, for a lot of reasons, not necessarily economic reasons, get into trouble with drugs or get arrested and have some emotional issues.

"Our approach at Best Friends is that any group that wants to come and participate in the rescue work is welcome to come. We have kids from the Genesis Youth Program, which is a court-ordered restitution program. We also have a project—Second Chance, out of Salt Lake City—that helps. These kids are more than welcome to come. We do have certain safety protocols and emotional protocols. We don't work with kids who have severe anger management issues, because it is hard for our staff to deal with, but other things are irrelevant. What is relevant to our staff is that the kids are going to be nice to the animals and help with the daily work and help with projects. If they are willing to do all that, then the staff will treat them like everyone else. So for a lot of these kids this is the first time in their life they have ever been accepted for something that is positive. They get lots of attention for negative things, but at the sanctuary nobody really cares where the kid came from, what they did, what they look like. These things are all irrelevant. If they are going to pitch in and help with the team, then they are part of the team. And that means a lot to the kids that come to us. A lot of healing happens and we see a lot of changes.

"When the kids come from the therapeutic program we get a lot of feedback. I have kids who have turned in their families for dog fighting. Just by being with us for a week, we have kids who are from dog fighting backgrounds and who are terrified of dogs on Monday, and by Friday they are walking any dog we give them. We invite them to come and be a part of everything we are doing. This demonstrates to them that they can be part of something in their lives that is worthwhile."

I asked Nathania what it was about the program, about being with the dogs that made such an impact on the lives of these children. Her answer brought me to tears because the concept is so simple yet so beautiful. "Most of the older dogs or very young dogs that we have just want attention," she told me. "The ones who interact with the volunteers are socialized to people. The older dogs who are ill or have injuries really touch these kids, and it touches them because we didn't euthanize them. We didn't throw them away, or send them someplace else. *It touches someplace in these kids who feel like they have been thrown away. . . .* They see us in our daily activities and in our daily commitment to animals that otherwise have been discarded because of age or illness or injury. They see us take care of three-legged dogs and deaf dogs or blind dogs or old dogs or young dogs that are very rambunctious.

"We talk about the young dogs—when they may have a scuffle in their runs with other dogs, we put them in time out. These kids know what time out means. That we might have to put a dog in isolation for a short time to sort out what the problem is—they understand that. That we still care about these animals and take care of them means a great deal to them. That we know them by name and that we know their stories, their feeding charts; their food is given out by name.

And they have their own place to eat in their runs. They are individualized and personalized. Then we take them down to the cemetery where the animals that have died in our care and they just get blown away that every animal, even in death, is known by name. It has a huge impact. It's the animals themselves but it is also our relationship with them and it is also allowing them to be part of it. Some of these kids come from homes and families where they are not allowed to be part of life."

During a visit to a local drug and alcohol rehabilitation center, Woody and Katie helped residents feel better for a while as they talked about the animals waiting for them at home. "Is this the 'dogs for drunks' program?" one man joked upon entering the day room and seeing the dogs. "I'm a cat person myself, but I miss having animals around." The men called Woody and Katie over to them and petted them, played with them and told stories of the dogs whom they had loved in their lives. When we visited the women's day room, the atmosphere was less festive and more therapeutic. The women gathered around Woody and Katie, all jostling for position so that they could pet them, hug them and offer love to these healers in fur coats who had come to visit them. "Do they need a bowl of water?" asked one woman. Then, catching herself, she joked, "Uh oh, there's my co-dependency coming out! I've been told I need to work on that!"

Animals fulfill a basic human need by offering unconditional love and affection. They make us feel needed and important by their dependence on us. They provide unfailing friendship and nonjudgmental companionship, and they have been proven to have the ability to keep us healthy and happy! Teaching children to be kind to animals, whether through formal lessons or simple visits, is the most important and effective way we have of repaying animals for all they do for us.

9

Voices from the Classroom

"If there is just one kid who gets something out of it, it's worth it."

—John Harvill, Middle School Teacher

I had been called to visit a middle school by a fifth-grade teacher with a great idea. "Could you set up in the media center for the entire day, and the whole fifth grade could visit at scheduled times during the day?" I thought it was a wonderful suggestion and jumped at the opportunity to spend the day with an entire inner-city fifth grade, approximately 175 students.

I had brought a Power Point presentation on spaying and

neutering. It was primarily a math lesson (statistics), with a spay/neuter message. The lesson consisted of various facts about the euthanasia rate in our country and encouraged students to conduct a survey of local shelters to find out whether they sterilize their animals prior to adoption, and to determine the effects of the shelters' policies on the local euthanasia rate. The presentation took about thirty-five minutes with a five-minute introduction and a ten-minute Q & A period built in at the end.

The students were seated in a horseshoe-shaped configuration and I was able to walk into the half-circle and make contact with each one. As I introduced myself and Woody and Katie, who had been patiently waiting to interact with the children, one little girl raised her hand. She was small for a fifth-grader, with straggly reddish-blonde hair and a waif-like aura about her.

"My dad throws my cat up against the door," she stated in a very quiet whisper. It was as if she had been told I was coming and was waiting to unburden herself. "Wow, that's bad!" I said. "How does that make you feel?" I asked her. "Really bad," she said in a thin voice. "So how do you think it makes your cat feel?" I asked her "She can take it," she said. "My dad says she can take it. . . . He does it when he gets mad." I told her that her cat should not have to take any kind of abuse and asked her what her mom did when this happened. "It makes her mad, but she can't stop him." This exchange was taking place quietly between us, and only the students to her immediate left and right could hear it. Woody and Katie had been working the room and were keeping the other students occupied. I turned to the teacher and told her what had just happened. "Yeah, it starts with the cat, the next thing is he'll be throwing you up against the door," she said to the girl. "Let's see if we can get you and your kitty some help." I continued with my lesson, but the idea of a poor, helpless cat cowering in a home nearby was on my mind. If this child believed her father, that the cat "could take it," then what else might he be teaching her?

Judy Johns of the Latham Foundation asserts that humane educators are morally and legally responsible for reporting any abuse or neglect they suspect is occurring. "A core concept of humane education is that all living things deserve love and attention. Humane educators validate this concept, and therefore they may represent hope for children who are not receiving adequate care, including those who are exposed to animal abuse or other forms of family violence. In this role, humane educators may be confronted with revelations of abuse. I believe they must report this abuse." The authors of *Teaching Compassion: A Guide for Humane Educators, Teachers and Parents* state: "If a child tells you a story about animal abuse, you should not ignore what you have heard. If you continue teaching as though nothing has happened, the children will feel that the story was not shocking and that you did not consider the animal abuse inappropriate. Without interventions, children may not learn any alternatives to repeating cruelty. . . . Humane education classes can do much more than teach children about pet care or habitat loss. They are an opportunity to intervene in the lives of troubled children, to teach new ways to deal with the abusive behaviors that surround them. . . ."[23]

The words of Dr. Randy Lockwood came back to me once again. "We never know what effect we have on these children's lives. We don't know what they are learning or not learning at home. A humane educator coming in to their classroom may be the only voice they ever hear telling them to be kind and compassionate to animals."

I wondered, though, why children would listen to me when their own parents are telling them something different. I decided to ask some teachers who have embraced the idea of humane education.

John Harvill and Jady Hill are two inner-city middle-school teachers who have their work cut out for them. They are both gentle and strong, with the powerful good looks of football players or ex-marines. They look like they can handle anything. Yet there have been days when I visit the classroom with the dogs and see the stress in their faces. They are the drop-out prevention teachers who inherit the students whom other teachers have given up on. Because their work is so challenging and their students so tough, I asked them to share their thoughts on humane education and how they thought it might have helped their hardened and cynical students.

"Definitely you can tell that there are some changes," says John, "because every week when you come with the dogs, first of all, even the kids that are kind of hard core, they still call the dogs over and like to play with them and pet them, and even if they are not paying attention to anything that is being taught, you can tell that at least they like playing with the dogs. They are getting something out of that interaction alone. Then there are some kids that if you brought a dog in you would have thought you were bringing in a giant green alien! You know, they are just not used to being around animals. But now, they are not so jittery. One boy told me right off the bat that he did not like animals and to 'keep that dog away from me,' and now when you come in he doesn't freak out. The dogs go over to him and he responds to them. The different animals coming in help kids to understand about animals and give them a better appreciation of animals.

I can see how happy some of these hardened, macho kids feel when dogs come in. It softens them right away. I can also see how it is when you don't come. I have kids in my class who say, 'Is the dog lady coming? Is the animal lady coming today?' If I say you are not coming they are visibly disappointed."

One week I brought Abby, a "Delta Dog in Training," to John and Jady's school. She is great with kids and has a friendly and outgoing temperament, but her obedience skills need to be honed. The students were accustomed to Woody and Katie (more sedate and dignified dogs don't exist). So when Abby, a two-year-old rescued yellow Lab, came to visit, the students got a kick out of her shenanigans. The students were delighted with Abby's charm and spirit, and it showed in their questions, their interactions with me as well as Abby, and their overall attitude toward the class. "It's kind of funny," said Jady. "The week you brought the dog that was a little hyper, ran around, the kids got into it a little more. It was funny to see these kids with the macho persona laughing and playing with her. They have these exteriors we just cannot penetrate, but Abby did. Some of the kids walk around like they are the meanest, toughest guys on the earth. I tell them all the time, there is nothing wrong with being polite or showing affection."

John appreciates the way humane education ties in with some of the character education activities he arranges for his students. For example, the children's uninhibited interaction with Abby reminded him of " . . . when we go on the prison tour, we got guys that are in there that talk to them and these guys are in there for life. They readily admit that they will never get to hug or kiss their own mothers again and that they would do anything to be able to do that. Here are these big, tough macho prisoners crying over not being able to hug their moms. I try to tell the kids that there is nothing wrong with them if they like dogs. It is not going to make them look like a sissy if they are playing with the dog." John also related the story of the time a sheriff's detective came to visit the classroom. "The officer talked about you and told the kids that the reason they should listen to you is because it could keep them out of trouble. She told them that if they think it is okay to kill squirrels with BB guns and torment and abuse cats and dogs, then eventually it could lead to more than that. She told them about how David Berkowitz, the Son of Sam, admitted to killing his neighbor's pets when he was a kid. How Jeffrey Dahmer tortured and killed frogs, cats and dogs as a child, then grew up to become one of the worlds' most despised serial killers. She taught them that animals are not made to be someone's punching bag. It is good that they are learning this at an early age."

John and Jady pointed out that most of their students do not have much of an education at home. They are not learning a lot about character, responsibility or citizenship, and they are certainly not learning about animals. "You are targeting a really good population. This school is in an economically disadvantaged area, where seventy-five percent of the students take advantage of the free lunch program. . . . These are the drop-out prevention classes so these are pretty hard core kids," says Jady. "I do a special education class and I work with emotionally handicapped kids, so there are kids who, if they see a dog, will most likely throw stuff at it, maybe even kick it. So we are educating a good population." John agreed, "I think they are getting the message. I have seen it myself, like when we go on field trips—we go to the park afterwards, and I have seen kids that will go to kill a lizard and these kids will say, 'Man, just leave the lizard alone. It's not bothering you,' whereas before you started coming, nobody spoke up for the animals."

There are some students in these classes who are fifteen years old, in the eighth grade and reading on a second grade reading level. Many of them cannot even perform simple multiplication. "So, really," says John, "the academics at this point are somewhat secondary. It's not like overnight they are going to flip a switch and all of a sudden start reading on an eighth-grade level. All this stuff that we do—humane education, other speakers, character education—they don't get any of this stuff at home. You don't have mothers and fathers telling their kids that some things are unacceptable. I used to tease lizards, and my father saw me one day and said, 'You are acting stupid, who does that? Don't do that, do something more constructive.' "

Jady agreed. "I have mothers tell me that they did crack while they were pregnant. We are starting to see these kids who were born in the late eighties whose mothers were on crack. One parent was actually telling me not to blame the disobedience on her daughter, that she was doing crack two weeks before she was born; her daughter was born addicted to drugs. We have a whole section in here where there are some parental concerns and some guidance problems and they are a step slow, a step behind, and they are just getting by. Being a teenager is hard. This is the toughest age right here. Kids trying to figure out where they fit in the world, what their role is, what is expected of them. Sometimes animals just give them a chance to be just a kid. No expectations."

John told me that he has talked to many teachers over the years. These are folks who teach in a variety of schools and connect with a range of students from the very successful to the deeply troubled. The differences abound, but there seems to be a common thread among all teachers. When they start teaching, they think they are going to help each and every kid, only to find out that they might help one, and that was a fluke! "Especially at this level," says John, "you may never find out the kid that you did help. They go into high school and you never see them again. You don't get to watch them graduate or hear about their plans—going to college, joining the military. Not a lot of kids at seventeen or eighteen say, "Let me go back and thank my seventh-grade teacher." My theory has always been, you plant a seed, and hopefully one day the seed will take root and grow. You never know if the seed you planted is the one that ended up growing or if it was someone else's seed." As humane educators dedicated to helping students develop character through interactions with animals, we can only hope that the seed that grows was planted by someone who has respect for the earth and all her creatures. I thought of Conrad,[24] a student in this class who is physically imposing and knows it. He's a tough guy who walks around like Jean Claude Van Damme. Interestingly, he was the only one who showed outward fear of the little red snake. Exposure to animals, humane education—this was all brand new to him. So when I visit next year, he'll meet Chance again, and maybe next time he sees a snake he will let it go. These are the seeds we plant.

I am always amazed at the revelation that the teachers, too, learn as a result of the humane education lessons. On his way to work on the morning of our interview, John had seen a dead cat on the street. He found himself thinking about how she might have died, who might have hit her and whether the driver had even stopped. "It used to be I wouldn't even see the cat, or if I did I wouldn't think twice about it. Now I am aware; I am thinking, 'How did this happen?" John also remembered Alyson Strange's lesson about snakes and their place in nature. When she visited his class, Alyson taught the students that snakes have a job to do in nature. "If you kill snakes," she told them, "you rob nature of the job that animal was put here to do." She explained that if there is a snake in your yard, there must be a food source, and that if you kill the snake, you are inviting trouble in the form of a rat or mouse infestation. "Ninety percent of the snake bites on record occurred because someone was trying to kill or capture a snake," said Alyson. "It's better to just leave them alone." "I have to be honest with you," John told me. "Before I heard that lesson about snakes, if I was doing yard work and I saw a snake, I would cut it in half with a shovel. Now I won't do that; I will just let it go. When I was a kid, mowing yards with my father, we came across snakes all the time, and we always killed them. We just always thought snakes were bad. We didn't realize that they were such a vital part of the ecosystem." Jady added that he, too, had seen some changes in his attitude. He related a conversation to me in which he told his dad, a farmer in the panhandle who routinely kills snakes, "Maybe you shouldn't be doing that." Fortunately for John and Jady's students, they were learning this lesson at an early age.

Although this classroom is populated with students at risk for dropping out of school, some of them are quite bright; their problems are mainly behavioral. One of these students is Giovanni, an African-American student who would like to work with animals someday. He's a small thirteen-year-old, quite handsome in his glasses. "There's a kid who, if he hadn't heard your message over the past two years, would probably do anything to an animal to impress the neighborhood kids," say Jady. "But now, I don't think he would. I remember that last year he was the one who always wanted to walk the dog down with you, help you out to the car. Now I think that if he was with a bunch of kids and they were teasing a dog or whatever—I don't think he has enough moxie in him to say, 'You guys need to stop,' because he's so small, but I bet he would have enough compassion to walk away from it, maybe tell someone or even tell the kids individually to leave the dog alone."

John adds, "With kids, it's easy to do the right thing when nobody's looking but it is hard to do the right thing when when their peers are around. They have a conscience but they won't do it when their friends are around. Most kids know, after a certain age, right from wrong."

During our interview, Giovanni had entered the room. He agreed to talk about his feelings on humane education. "Most of the kids like coming here for your class. Even if they are not interested in the talking part, they like the animals. But I don't care what the kids think; I like animals and I want to be a veterinarian when I grow up and that's what I want to learn about. I decided halfway through the year last year, after you had been coming a while, that I wanted to be a vet."

Karen Davis, Ph.D, founder and director of United Poultry Concerns, does not doubt the importance of humane education. She tells the story of an acquaintance of hers who changed the direction of his life because of something he had learned in college.

"Dr. Eldon Kienholz was a full professor of poultry and nutritional science at Colorado State University. He had come from a farming background. Not only did he grow up raising animals for food, but, he explained, subsequently shooting every animal in sight because farmers regarded animals as pests or vermin to be eliminated. Not only was he not chastised for killing squirrels and all kinds of animals as part of his everyday life, but he was encouraged.

"When Eldon went to college he took a Peace Studies course. It had nothing to do with animals. The concept of peace at that time in the 1940s did not include our relationship to other animals and the earth, but peace among humans. He learned pacifist ideas—non-aggression, respect for others and not being one to inflict pain and suffering. He learned about not imposing your will upon others arbitrarily and unjustly. The peace studies course emphasized respect for fellow human beings.

"He went on to become a professor of poultry science for the University of Colorado. He conducted horrible experiments, as all poultry scientists do, on chickens and turkeys. He burned off their tails and wings in an attempt to determine whether the birds not having those appendages could save fifteen percent in feed costs to the industry. He conducted other experiments along those lines. In the course of his career he began to have a resurgence of memories. He began to doubt the work he was doing. One of the most important contributors to this doubt was his memory of the peace studies course that he had taken as a young college student. He began to remember some of the ideas and concepts that he had forgotten for decades. These ideas came back into his consciousness and he compared those ideas with the cruelties that he inflicted on birds as the very essence of his career. It was the peace studies course that nagged at him and served as a kind of criticism in his consciousness as to what he was doing to make a living. And he was making a good living. As he explained, the peace course he took did not include nonhuman animals or considerations outside the human species, but he saw those links and made those connections, and he became so fraught with guilt and a sense of moral wrongness in his work that he chose to retire from his tenured position early. He did not want to continue to be a poultry scientist and do the kinds of things that he had to do in order to stay in his profession."

There is little doubt that a seed is planted somewhere along the line. For a professor who grew up as a child hurting animals to suddenly forsake his career there had to be a powerful force. For a child to tell an educator that something she taught him has inspired him to make a decision about his future is a gratifying and heartwarming experience. As John Harvill says, if you get through to one kid, it makes it all worthwhile.

I think Giovanni will make an excellent animal doctor someday.

10

The Birds and the Bees

"As the birds do love the spring, or the bees their careful king . . ."

—From "Diaphenia" by Henry Constable

I casually drop a laminated photo of an adorable, fluffy dog on Bobby's desk. I tell him, "This is your dog. He's very sweet and loving, but he runs away a lot. He got out of the yard and went over to Suzy's house. .." (here, I drop another photo on Suzy's desk) " . . . where he 'made friends' with her female dog. Sixty-three days later, Suzy has a litter of puppies . . ." (I drop six to eight photos on her desk as I say this) " . . . and she must find homes for them all. Who is responsible for those puppies?" I ask. "Bobby? Suzy?" I pick up some of the photos and distribute them around the classroom. A puppy here, a puppy there. I repeat the scenario again and again until almost all the students in the class have at least one puppy. Now the fun starts. The puppies keep coming but everyone already has one or more. What do we do with the surplus? Give them to me—I work at the shelter; I can find homes. So I take a few handfuls of puppies back, but guess what! Everyone in the room has puppies; nobody wants any more. Sadly, I drop them one by one into a brown paper bag marked "PTS" (put to sleep).

Lisa Cushing, of the National Association of Humane and Environmental Education, offers another version of this activity wherein she places photos of houses on the walls and windows around the classroom. The 8 x 10, laminated photos sport Velcro spots. Her dog photos also have Velcro spots, and she gives the class a few minutes to find homes for their dogs by affixing the photos to the spots on the houses. Sadly, inevitably, there are many left. Then, she reveals a much larger photo of an animal shelter with many Velcro spots, and the students who haven't found homes for their dogs can bring them to the shelter. But again, some are left over, and it is up to the students to figure out what happens to them.

Either way, *they get the point.*

It is lessons such as this one that bring home the fact that those who do not sterilize their animals are contributing to a problem others must deal with. There are many ways to get this point across and a variety of recommended videos and books to help. But interactive play is an exceptionally inspired way to get kids' attention and help them to understand that they can effect change, even as kids. If given the facts of the result of failure to sterilize, obedience train and keep animals close, children will not only come up with solutions, but will become more empowered to effect change in their own neighborhoods. Thus, we are not telling them what to do; we are showing them the tragic results we have obtained so far and asking them to find solutions to existing problems.

So at what age can we begin to teach children about overpopulation and sterilization? Certainly, if they are not educated in the ways of reproduction, they cannot be expected to learn about sterilization. I have found that third grade is about the time we can begin to discuss spaying and neutering in a superficial way. In middle school, we can discuss more detailed ideas such as early-age sterilization, consequences of failure to sterilize both for the animal and for the community, adoption from a shelter versus purchase from a pet store, and ways to help bring others to accept that sterilization is a good thing for all concerned. In high school, we can discuss more advanced topics, such as legislation to mandate sterilization, unique campaigns to help educate the public, and the movement toward a no-kill nation.

Woody's Wisdom/The Pet Suitcase (see chapter seven) is a good start for younger students, because it educates them about our responsibilities toward animals, but it is much too juvenile for children in grades three and up. Ann Gearhart of the Snyder Foundation has developed a wonderful lesson plan that involves the spay/neuter stamp and is interactive and far-reaching. One reason teachers like it is that it helps them teach the required skill of writing personal and business letters.

Education Initiatives for the Spay/Neuter Stamps and Snyder Foundation for Animals Pen Pal Program

Goal

To create a better understanding of companion animals in our society by using the American Partnership for Pets Spay/Neuter Stamps and the Snyder Foundation Pen Pal Program

Objectives

1. Students will write at least two letters that convey information regarding animals, and request a response, through the Pen Pal correspondence program.
2. Using the Spay/Neuter stamps, students will mail letters to cities across the United States, then collect responses and identify locations of postmarks on a U.S. map.
3. Students will create a class journal of photographic images of animals, to be shared at school or on a field trip to a Pen Pal school.

Activities

- Receive a cancelled postmark from each state. Obtain a standard, classroom size map of the United States. As you receive the envelope with the cancelled stamp, place the stamp in or near the appropriate state.
- Collect the cancelled Spay/Neuter stamps to "measure" the amount of correspondence received.
- Establish a Pen Pal Program with a neighboring school by asking a willing teacher to have his or her students exchange letters with yours. The optimal goal of this activity could be a field trip to the correspondent's school.
- Introduce the hobby of stamp collecting. Invite a collector to do a presentation for your students.
- Create a mock stamp and cancellation device for in-school mailing from class to class.

- As an art and social awareness activity, design a stamp on different animal issues.
- Create a class journal of animal pictures from newspapers, magazines, websites and other print media. Limit the size to 8 1/2 by 11 so the pictures will fit into a standard 3-ring binder. For each picture, include information regarding the source, publication and date, and the reason for selecting the picture. For the sake of longevity, consider sliding the pictures into an economy-weight plastic sleeve.
- Encourage students to correspond or "pen pal" with friends and relatives.
- Create a writing activity for students to inform others about the social awareness issue behind the Spay/Neuter stamps: to benefit you, your pet, and the community.
- Create a writing activity for students to persuade others to use the Spay/Neuter stamps.
- Create a writing activity for students to express their point of view on the Spay/Neuter stamps.
- If possible, access the American Partnership for Pets website and links to each member of the Partnership to see the wide range of work being done across the country to benefit companion animals.
- Obtain replicas of other related, inexpensive stamp materials from such companies as Kenmore (1-800-225-5059 Mon–Fri 8-5 EST, www.KenmoreStamp.com) and Mystic Stamp Co. (1-800-433-7811, www.mystic-stamp.com).
- Contact the United States Postal Service at www.usps.com. The Postal Bulletin has devoted a great deal of space to the Spay/Neuter Stamps.
- Plan a trip to a Post Office near your school.
- Invite a humane educator to visit your school and provide

a program related to animal welfare issues and the Spay/Neuter Stamps.

- As an extension activity, consult the Project WILD curriculum and activity guide, published through the Council for Environmental Education, and enjoy their Wildlife on Coins and Stamps activity.

These activities can be modified to accommodate many grade levels. Because students have an innate interest in animals, the Spay/Neuter Stamps and Pen Pal program lend themselves well to a meaningful hands-on academic experience and a straightforward approach to a social awareness issue.

The following program for elementary school children can involve an entire school district (or perhaps certain zones within your school district). Teachers love to lend their support to contests that incorporate math and writing and give kids a chance to win prizes, too.

Mona's Kittens Contest

For purposes of this contest question we are assuming certain facts. The facts of this contest are:

- Mona is a cat.
- Mona is not spayed.*
- Mona will become pregnant three (3) times a year for each year she lives.
- Mona will have eight (8) kittens during each pregnancy.
- Each of Mona's kittens will live ten years.

- *Spay–a simple surgery to remove Mona's ability to have kittens

Part One
How many kittens will Mona have in her lifetime (which we will approximate at ten years for the sake of this problem)?

Part Two
One half of Mona's kittens are females. Assume the same set of facts for each one of these females. What is the total number of kittens Mona and all her kittens will have in their lifetime?

How to Win
After completing Parts One and Two, choose one of the following:

1. Write a 500-word answer to this question: What part does the Humane Society or local shelter play in helping the community to reduce stray or unwanted animals?

2. Design a poster that shows Mona and all her many, many kittens.

You may first decide to hold this contest in one class or grade level. Or you may take on the entire school district—and that's not as big a task as it may seem. In order to kick off a contest that involves an entire school district you must first obtain permission. This is easily done with a letter to the school district outlining the contest and explaining deadline, prizes and logistics. Once you obtain permission, you can advertise the contest in teachers' newsletters or through direct mailing or posters in staff lounges. Set a deadline, typically four to five months after the kickoff. Be aware of any standardized testing that may be taking place during the school year and try to avoid that time frame. Teachers are not going to support a contest during standardized testing months.

Veterinary clinics and shelters will be your best bet for sponsors for prizes. Send letters to local vets, pet stores that do not sell animals, groomers or other animal-oriented businesses to find sponsors for prizes. The prizes can be trophies, ribbons, awards, books or animal-related gift baskets. Having a small party for the class that participated the most is fun and brings you into the classroom for a humane education lesson. I always reward teachers who have encouraged their students to participate with a subscription to *KIND News*, a publication of the National Association for Humane and Environmental Education (NAHEE). This age-appropriate newspaper comes out every month, and teachers receive thirty-two copies to share with their class. This valuable and popular resource includes teacher worksheets and lesson plans and is available for $30 in Primary, Junior and Senior editions.

Another way to have fun with elementary school students and teach lessons about animals is through drama. Puppets, especially, take on personalities and offer a great deal of fun, mixing education and playtime. Puppets are available online or in thrift stores. They don't have to be expensive or new, and the types of animals are not as important as the things the animals have to say. Here is a script to get you started on a puppet play. I'll bet you can write one too!

Pet Store Puppet Play

This scene can be played out by volunteers from the class or by one or more educators. It teaches children several valuable lessons about what happens to animals when they are no longer cute and cuddly.

Characters
HUMAN puppet
MOUSE puppet
DOG puppet or stuffed dog

Stage left: Small box containing a DOG. *Sign that reads "Pet Store" over box.*

Stage right: HUMAN *puppet enters, sees dog in box and begins singing. If the* DOG *is a puppet, his tail can wag during the song.*

HUMAN: How much is that doggie in the window,
The one with the waggely tail?
How much is that doggie in the window?
I do hope that doggie's for sale.

MOUSE *puppet appears behind* HUMAN *puppet.*

MOUSE: Oh no! You don't mean that!

HUMAN: What?

MOUSE: You don't mean that you would buy a dog from a pet store, do you?

HUMAN: Why not?

MOUSE: Because puppies in pet stores come from puppy mills and they are horrible places! They're like puppy factories! It's terrible, it's awful! And if you buy a puppy from the pet store, then they will just get another one from the puppy mill and keep selling them. You don't want to give them your business, do you? Not after what they do to the dogs!
HUMAN: But he looks so sad and lonely.

MOUSE: They want you to think that! They want you to feel sorry for them! They count on that! They count on them looking lonely and they know if you feel really sorry for them you will buy one. But don't fall for it! Don't do it!

HUMAN: Wow, I didn't know that pet stores that sell puppies get them from such horrible places. I am really glad you stopped me. I wouldn't want to play any part in all of that!

MOUSE: No! And look how expensive they are! Puppies in pet stores are much more expensive than if you get your puppy from a shelter or even from a nice person who has puppies to find homes for. I am really glad you aren't going to buy that puppy! *(To the audience.)* Boys and girls! Aren't you glad that _____(HUMAN) isn't going to get his puppy from the pet store?

Curtain closes, then opens to show a sign that reads "Six months later."

Stage left: Same DOG *in same box, only the sign on the box now says "Animal Shelter."*

Stage right: HUMAN *puppet enters, sees the* DOG *and approaches.*

HUMAN: Hey, I know you! You are the same doggie I saw in the window! I saw you six months ago! What are you doing here?

DOG: A family bought me for Christmas! They brought me home and made a really big fuss over me! They played with me all day long, and gave me lots of toys and plenty to eat!

HUMAN: Wow, that sounds like a great life you had!

DOG: Yeah, but after awhile, everyone stopped talking to me. Nobody played with me anymore. They tied me up outside! Even when it was raining! Even when it was really,

really hot! Even when it was snowing and it was really, really cold! They had me tied up outside all day long and nobody talked to me. I barked and barked but still nobody talked to me.

HUMAN: That's awful! What did you do that was bad?

DOG: I don't know! That's the thing. I really don't know what I did that was so bad that they tied me up outside. Then one day, they said I was going for a ride in the car and here I am! Now I'm here in this cage!

HUMAN: I have an idea! Why don't you come home with me? Maybe you can come live with me and we can be a family, would you like that?

DOG: Woof! Woof! That means YES!

HUMAN: It's settled then! You've got a new best friend and so do I!

MOUSE puppet enters.

MOUSE: Well, boys and girls, did you like the way the story ended? Isn't it wonderful that our puppy found a home after all? What might have happened if ______(HUMAN) had not come to the shelter that day? Where could the dog possibly have ended up? What did we learn about pet stores? What if the family had taken the dog to obedience school instead of tying him up outside? How do you think the dog felt when he was left out in the cold or hot weather? Is it fair to tie a dog up outside?

Here is another play script, but that's all I will give you! Your creativity and love for animals will have you writing your own puppet scripts in no time.

Lost Dog Puppet Play

I use a variety of animal puppets for this play, but you may use whatever animal puppets you have.

Characters

SMALL TOAD
PUPPY
MOM (larger toad)
DR. ELEPHANT (elephant puppet dressed as a doctor)
MOUSE
CAT
VETERINARY CLINIC RECEPTIONIST (any animal or human puppet)

SMALL TOAD *and* PUPPY *enter, stage left.* SMALL TOAD *is singing to the tune of "I'm Bringing Home a Baby Bumblebee."*

SMALL TOAD:I'm bringing home a puppy dog today.
I think that he must have lost his way,
So I'm bringing home a puppy dog today—
(spoken) Oh! I wonder what Mom will say.

MOM enters, stage right.

SMALL TOAD: Mom, I found this little lost dog. We need to help him, Mom! *(urgently)* What should we do?!

MOM: Good job, son! I always told you we should help others in need if we can. Good boy. *(Looking at dog)* Are you lost, little dog? You have no collar—we don't know your name! Guess we should take him to the vet and see what Dr. Elephant says.

Curtain closes, then opens to show DR. ELEPHANT, PUPPY,

SMALL TOAD *and* MOM *standing beneath a sign that says "Veterinary Clinic."*

DR. ELEPHANT: Well, Mrs. Toad, it's a good thing you brought him in. He looks like he's been lost a long time. Leave him with me and I'll let you know what happens.

SMALL TOAD: Will you take good care of him?

DR. ELEPHANT: Oh yes. We'll give him some lunch and a nice flea bath. . . . He'll be fine!

Curtain closes, then opens to show MOUSE, *walking back and forth and wringing his hands, singing.* CAT *enters during song.*

MOUSE: Oh where, oh where has my little dog gone?
Oh where, oh where can he be?
Oh where, oh where has my little dog gone?
(spoken) I hope he comes home to me.

CAT: Oh, Marty Mouse, I'm so sorry you lost your little dog. I can help you find him. Was he wearing a tag?

MOUSE: No, I took it off because I was giving him a flea bath, but when I went to get the shampoo, he was gone.

CAT: Oh, my. Well, first we'll make signs and put them out all over the neighborhood. Then we will call all the vets in town, and the police and the animal rescue league. Maybe they know where he is. Let's get to work. You make the signs. I'll call the vet.

MOUSE: Okay, thanks, Phoebe. Thanks for being my friend. *Curtain closes, opens in Veterinary Clinic to show* RECEPTIONIST *answering telephone.*

RECEPTIONIST: Doctor's office, may I help you? Oh yes,

we have a little brown puppy dog. Yes, he was brought in this morning. Oh yes, he's fine. You can come right over and get him. *(Calling offstage, to* DR. ELEPHANT*)* The puppy's dad just called—he's coming to get him.

DR. ELEPHANT *enters with* PUPPY.

DR. ELEPHANT: Wonderful, we just finished his bath. *(To* PUPPY.*)* Hear that, little dog? You're going home.

CAT *and* MOUSE *enter and see* PUPPY, *who wags his tail.* MOUSE *runs to hug him.*

MOUSE: Elvis! I was so worried about you! Thank you, Doctor. How did he get here?

DR. ELEPHANT: Mrs. Toad and her little boy brought him in. They were very worried about him.

Curtain closes, then opens to show MOUSE, SMALL TOAD *and* MOM *alone onstage.*

MOUSE: Thank you, Teddy Toad, for finding Elvis. He could have been kidnapped or hit by a car! Or a bully could have teased him, or he could have ended up far, far away! But you saved him.

SMALL TOAD: Aw, gee, I'm so happy we got him home.

MOUSE: Well Teddy Toad, I am going to reward you with a Tofutti Cutie! I wish more boys and girls would help little puppies when they have lost their way. I love Elvis and I would miss him terribly if he didn't come home. Thank you, you're a hero, for you saved a life today. *(*PUPPY *licks* SMALL TOAD's *face).*

(To audience.) I think Teddy Toad deserves a big round of

applause, don't you? What might have happened to Elvis if Teddy had not taken him to the vet? What should I do to make sure that Elvis does not get lost again? What are some of the ways we can make sure our animals are identified? Where are some other places we can take lost animals? What are some things we can do to help lost animals find their way home?

The lessons described above are only a few of the ways we can involve children in stopping the euthanasia of millions of animals every year across the country. Wouldn't it be wonderful if we could empower today's generation to find solutions to making our country a no-kill nation? Children are capable of understanding complex ideas and can voice them in a simple and innocent way. Sometimes they can do this much better than adults can. During a summer camp program for elementary-school kids, I asked the group to raise their hands if they knew what spay/neuter meant. One boy, Antwan, who frequently accompanies his aunt, a veterinary technician, to work, raised his hand. In a loud and clear voice, Antwan declared that "spaying is when a veterinarian removes a female's ovaries and uterus, and neutering is when the vet removes the testicles." A hush fell over the room as the children glanced nervously at one another. I peeled myself off the ceiling long enough to ask the group if anyone understood what Antwan had just said. To my utter surprise, most of them did. I restated the definition anyway, saying that spaying and neutering removes an animals' ability to have puppies or kittens or contribute to the making of puppies or kittens. Antwan's answer was right, innocent and direct. Kids appreciate that we don't insult them with baby talk or cute words for body parts or medical procedures. Once, when a smart-aleck high school kid challenged me on the need to neuter his dog, I informed him in no uncertain terms that dogs cannot and do not masturbate and therefore cannot release any pent-up energy in this way. He looked at me for a long moment and, in his first sincere moment since I had arrived, said "Thank you. I understand."

I believe in the adage that when the student is ready, the teacher will appear. I hope you will appear often and in a variety of classrooms and venues. The students are definitely ready.

11

Taking Animal Cruelty Seriously

> "One of the most dangerous things that can happen to a child is to kill or torture an animal and get away with it."
>
> —Margaret Mead, anthropologist

As a society, we want to do what we can to stop animal cruelty. Why? The reasons vary from wanting to protect the animals for their own sake to wanting to protect society from future acts of violence. And while it has not been proven that someone who commits acts of animal cruelty will then go on to commit violent acts against people, we do know that animal cruelty is often considered to be the beginnings of violent or abhorrent behavior. "People who have a propensity to harm or torture or kill animals in childhood generally are acting out or reacting to the witnessing of violence in their own lives and often begin to abuse animals for a variety of reasons," says Lt. Sherry Schlueter, Section Supervisor with the Broward County Sheriff's Office in Fort Lauderdale, Florida. "These reasons may include establishing power and control in their own lives by harming or killing another being that is vulnerable, or more vulnerable than they. . . . [The] animal is just the earliest victim because of its availability, its inability to report on its own behalf or testify or remove itself from jeopardy."

As section leader of the Special Victims and Family Crimes Section, Lt. Schlueter supervises a unique investigative unit that addresses the abuse, neglect and exploitation of animals, children, disabled adults and the elderly. She admits that there may be some instances in which animal cruelty can actually lead to human violence later. "Say, for example, there is a child who is not a victim of abuse or violence or witnessing that, but then is taken to a dog fight and acquires an affection for the blood sport and then begins to engage in it himself or herself. That exposure to that violence, those acts of violence themselves may have initiated the future behavior, but that is a rare case. Most of the things we talk about when we talk about the link or the cycle of violence have to do with a person who has witnessed or who is subjected to violence and then begins to act out. Unfortunately, there are those who are damaged by violence and cruelty themselves . . . [and] knowing that the animal is capable of suffering is what gives them the pleasure in the harming and torturing. [These] people are psychopathic and sociopathic; they lack conscience and are indifferent to all that. We can't change those people. They are broken and unfixable. But what we can do is stop the continuation of that."

Lt. Schlueter believes that attitudes in law enforcement regarding animal cruelty have changed dramatically. "I remember a time when cops didn't know that there were laws on the books; that's the whole reason that I became one! I remember when there would never be jail time for an animal cruelty case, when prosecutors wouldn't file cases that were presented because there was no precedent for it, and when judges would say in open court, 'I am not going to convict this person of animal cruelty and give him a criminal record simply because he beat some dog to death.' I remember those days, and they still exist, though not so much in the more enlightened counties. There are still judges, prosecutors, law enforcement professionals who don't get it and who think that this is stupid and they dismiss it from consideration."

Why the changes? "I give credit to the media coverage of animal cruelty cases that helps to educate and elevate expectations within the community," says Lt. Schlueter. "Because if society did not frown on these things then there would be no enforcement, no laws, no prosecution. There would only be escalation of violence. But when the public cares, a vocal public, the rest of society reacts in accordance, because most of government serves the public. The public *makes* it matter, so it does."

Dr. Randall Lockwood, Ph.D., is the force behind a critical program of the Humane Society of the United States (HSUS) called First Strike. Working with the Federal Bureau of Investigation (FBI), HSUS released a study in 1986 entitled "The Tangled Web of Abuse," which details evidence that those who abuse animals, especially those who begin at an early age, will go on to abuse people. Indeed, Jeffrey Dahmer, Kip Kinkel and the Columbine killers (and many more) all had a history of animal abuse. "But nowhere is animal cruelty more prevalent than behind closed doors," says Dr. Lockwood. "With little concern for consequences, abusers mistreat family pets for a variety of reasons." Some of the reasons animals are mistreated at the hands of abusive individuals include:

- To demonstrate and confirm power and control over the family
- To isolate the victim and children
- To force the family to keep family violence a secret
- To teach submission
- To retaliate for acts of independence and self-determination
- To perpetuate the context of terror
- To prevent a victim from leaving or coerce the victim to return
- To degrade the victim through involvement in the abuse

Intentional abuse differs from other crimes committed against animals in that abusing animals exposes the deliberateness of battering rather than loss of control. The abuse of animals and children is closely related, because both targets are small and vulnerable.

"The principles behind the First Strike program warn us that cruelty has interchangeable victims—whether it's animals, children, or adults abused in a domestic setting," says Wayne Pacelle, HSUS Senior Vice President of Communications and Government Affairs. "Similarly, kindness works in the same way; people who are kind to animals will more likely exhibit compassion toward other people." Wayne believes this "is the basis of the statutes that mandate humane education—understanding the connection between the victims of violence and trying to instill humane values at an early age. These are not radical or innovative or far-out ideas. They are fundamental, conservative and commonsensical. They are the ideas that help to create a humane society."

Now that we have learned about the effects of cruelty to animals and the potential for future harm to humans, we need to convince those in our community. As humane educators, we can do this. Margaret Mead, quoted at the beginning of this chapter, also said, "Never doubt that a small group of people cannot change the world, indeed, it is the only thing that has." You, and a few of your friends, can help change attitudes about animal cruelty.

Fortunately, we are not alone in our quest to reach out to social workers, prosecutors, journalists, police officers, educators and students about the rules for our relationship with animals. Several of the large national organizations and not a few smaller ones are leading the charge against cruelty to animals.

HSUS's First Strike Campaign is one of my favorites because it is easy to incorporate, and I have personally found HSUS to be extremely helpful and generous with their publications, information and expertise. The First Strike Campaign offers a traveling workshop that helps educators inform their communities of the link between animal cruelty and family violence. It helps local law enforcement, prosecutors, educators, social workers and others to carry out the initial strike against family violence by bringing them together to share resources, statistics and remedies. As a humane educator in the community, you may be interested in sponsoring one of these workshops. It's a manageable undertaking and will be well worth your time.

October is National Domestic Violence Awareness Month, so that may be a good time to plan a First Strike Conference. The idea of First Strike is to begin looking at the earliest indicators of family violence, so that we are positioned to effect an anticipatory strike against it. And experts have determined that one of the earliest indicators of family violence is animal abuse. Simply put, those who beat the family pet are most likely to abuse other family members, too—if not now, then soon. And by identifying those abusers, treating and/or punishing them and finding safe haven for the victims, we are effectively preempting the almost certain violence to come.

The First Strike workshops are effective in helping to raise awareness of the link between animal cruelty and family violence, but no single event can treat a social illness as devastating as domestic violence, so there should be post-conference plans to support victims who fear for the lives of their companion animals if they flee for their own safety. Since twenty-eight percent of the women who call shelter hotlines refuse to seek safety for themselves if it means leaving their pets behind, it stands to reason that programs set up to help battered women are not meeting all their needs. While battered women and children seek shelter from the storm of domestic violence, you may find someone willing to set up a foster network to give them peace of mind and their animals care and comfort until a permanent solution can be found for both. The First Strike Conference will address this project as well.

Here are some step-by-step instructions for putting on

your own First Strike conference (for more information, visit www.hsus.org).

Set your date! Make sure you have about four to six months' lead time to line up your speakers. In my experience, you can get maximum turnout by scheduling the event for a Saturday.

Line up your speakers. You may wish to invite speakers from the Humane Society of the United States (HSUS), your local county sheriff's office, your local Governors Task Force on Domestic Violence or State Attorney's office, and perhaps a veterinary or animal control panel. Your speakers list should include counselors or attorneys in the private sector. Other speakers are available from the Snyder Foundation for Animals and the Latham Foundation, Psychologists for the Ethical Treatment of Animals (PSYETA) and the Doris Day Animal League. All of these organizations and more have talented speakers on the subject of animal cruelty and domestic violence. Local activists may have their own access to experts from other animal agencies that have successfully initiated programs to assist animal victims of family violence. One year, I included a victim of domestic violence who had left her husband after he held a gun to her head. When she left, he drowned her cats in retaliation. Her story has been told on *Entertainment Tonight* and in *Cat Fancy* magazine. Working with local battered women's groups, you may meet a woman who has a similar story and is willing to share it. Most speakers will not charge a fee, but you may have to pay to reimburse them for their travel expenses. Airlines may donate the airfare, and local hotels, in exchange for putting their name on the flier, may offer a free night's lodging.

Find a venue. You should not have to pay for the room. Try government offices, churches and even condo meeting rooms. The local hospital may have a classroom they are willing to allow you to use, and even your local animal care agency may offer a classroom. Plan for about a hundred people.

Find a printer. Make up your fliers and ask a local printer to waive the printing and/or copying costs in exchange for putting their name on the fliers as a sponsor. Ask your local animal control agency or humane society if they will sponsor the event by doing the mass mailing for you. Your regional HSUS headquarters will gladly send out fliers in your state to all interested parties. Also, find sponsors in the form of local business owners who may be willing to donate stamps and/or mailing costs. And don't forget the power of e-mail.

Who should attend? Be sure to send fliers to local law enforcement officers, domestic violence workers, prosecutors, educators, social workers, animal control agencies and other members of the community who are committed to stopping animal abuse and domestic violence. Contact your local bar association, mental health centers, school boards and nursing licensing agency to learn how to offer continuing education units for your event. These units are needed by certain professionals to keep their license current and are sure to generate interest. You will find that the workshop is about more than just learning about animal abuse; it's also an occasion to meet others who share our goal of stopping violence in its many forms. Indeed, for years, government agencies and humane organizations have been searching for a way to find solutions together. This is the answer.

If a large, one-day conference is not your forte you may want to create a smaller version of this workshop and then offer it to high school students, civic groups and your local law enforcement and district attorney agencies. Working with a Power Point presentation or even transparencies, you can produce your own one-hour program that will be in great demand once the word gets out. Using the First Strike video, or one of the other videos such as the ones available from the Latham Foundation, PSYETA or the American Humane Association, you can put together a professional and effective presentation. Handouts and other materials are available free or for a small fee, or they can be copied or downloaded from a variety of websites. Offer your presentation to local domestic violence organizations, too.

PSYETA has a wonderful program that I have been able to incorporate called Anicare. Using their video, *Beyond Violence: The Human-Animal Connection*, I have been able to reach students and social workers and engage them in a discussion of the link between animal cruelty and violence to people. The video does feature some graphic images of animal abuse, but these are countered with tender, loving interactions between people and animals. Their video is touching and has a voiceover that is soothing and gentle, but the words make a strong impression; well-known figures such as Alice Walker and Jane Goodall discuss their own feelings about our relationship with animals. The video comes with a discussion guide that will assist you in facilitating a discussion for all venues and is sure to make an impact on anyone who is present.

Your audience for these presentations is ready made, because social workers and domestic violence workers are all responsible for continuing education in their field, and those who set up those programs are always looking for current and relevant ideas. Keep in mind that the laws are on your side because animal cruelty is a crime, at least a misdemeanor, in all fifty states, and some forms of animal cruelty are considered felonies in at least twenty-seven states. There is no controversy here. It's a matter of law.

Bringing a First Strike conference to your area will enhance your image as well. Dr. Lockwood describes some of the collateral benefits of bringing First Strike's message to your community: "What we are hearing from many humane organizations that have co-sponsored First Strike is that their involvement in the First Strike project has been a source of change of the perception of their organization and the acceptance of humane education efforts in their community. They relate stories of changes in the perception of established humane groups from just being 'animal' agencies to being organizations that care about families including animals, and about domestic violence affecting both animals and people. Addressing violence in all its forms has often led to the inclusion of representatives of humane groups in domestic violence councils and committees and has opened doors for them. It increases their credibility among community leaders, grantors, law enforcement, media, judges, and state and local legislators. We have always asserted that animal care and control is as vital to communities as police, libraries, schools and social service agencies, and I think it is the public awareness of the efforts of humane organizations in this arena that has helped jumpstart the popularity and message of First Strike."

Dr. Lockwood explained how his office has been repeatedly assured that their visits to towns across America have helped humane organizations change the perception of their groups and has facilitated dialogues with judges, social services and law enforcement. "In addition to bringing First Strike workshops to communities, we have been involved with other things such as the Governors Summit on Domestic Violence in Florida, and other important collaborations, because government is beginning to understand the importance of taking animal cruelty seriously and how doing so can create a less violent society all around. We are being taken very seriously by social service agencies and anyone who is trying to stop violence in their community. By virtue of our involvement with First Strike, we have been getting more and more involved in the field of adult protective services as well. Our office received a call a while back from a social service agency in North Dakota. They were very concerned about an elderly woman who was hoarding cats. They had called the National Center on Elder Abuse hotline and been given our number. This is unprecedented. This is a new awareness. And it is because of the efforts of human educators to bring First Strike and [to reveal] the connection between animal cruelty and family violence, mental illness and other issues that has brought this change about."

Bring the change you want to see to your world, too. Animal protection is no longer simply about protecting animals—it's also about protecting children, the elderly and other vulnerable populations. And it's about time. The next chapter shows us one reason why.

12

Are Your Students Committing a Crime?

"People who hurt animals are not nice people. These are people with a pattern of offensive behaviors, often violent."

—Dr. Randall Lockwood, Vice President for Research and Educational Outreach for the Humane Society of the United States

One of the biggest challenges facing humane educators, from urban schools to Indian reservations, is the ever-growing phenomenon of dog fighting. Linda Jo Fields Horse, a Native American living on the Winnebago Tribe reservation in Nebraska, sees blood sports used as an antidote to boredom and poverty. Dr. MaryAnn Jones, interviewed earlier in this book, explains that dog fighters project their desires to appear strong, powerful and aggressive onto their dogs. "[They] only think, 'Make 'em mean, make 'em mean.' They are projecting. That is why wrestling is so hugely popular. Fans are projecting strength and power and control and aggression. Like a child playing with action figures. . . . 'Mine is bigger than yours. My dog is bigger than yours'. . . . And then we justify it: 'This animal, this mean, tough pit bull, will bring me money, so that justifies my abusing this dog.' "

Fighting dogs has become such an enormous industry that humane educators must address it in their own backyards, city by city, community by community. In a survey of humane educators from all over the country, dog fighting was found to be second only to dog bites in areas to which humane educators devote most of their energy. In an effort to learn more about this disturbing trend that seems to be gaining in popularity, I convinced a judge to allow me to interview a convicted dog fighter.

When twenty-year-old "Alvin" was arrested and convicted of animal fighting, he was sentenced to community service at a local animal shelter. While Arin, the volunteer coordinator, was dead set against allowing Alvin to discharge his responsibility at our shelter (and rightly so; we had rehabilitating pit bulls to consider), I took up Alvin's cause and placed a call to his probation officer, his judge and finally Alvin himself. All agreed that Alvin would be allowed to complete his community service hours with our help only if he consented to sit down for a one-on-one interview with me so that I could learn about this cruel blood sport and the people who were drawn to it. My intention was to share this knowledge with local police agencies, animal control officers and, of course, humane educators. Having been inside the mind of a dog fighter makes it easier to relate to the kids who may be involved in this activity. I now have a deeper understanding of what motivates them, why they do what they do. What follows is an excerpt of Alvin's interview.

Michelle: When did you first get exposed to dogfighting?

Alvin: Like, I'm twenty right now, probably when I was fourteen.

Michelle: How?

Alvin: Me and my friend we used to always, we used to always have dogs, right, so what we used to do is walk the dogs around and I guess we just got to fighting the dogs. . . .

Michelle: What kind of dogs did you have?

Alvin: Ah, pit bulls.

Michelle: You started out with them?

Alvin: Yeah.

Michelle: How come you got them?

Alvin: I just had those type of dogs—

Michelle: So you got them with the intention of doing this?

Alvin: No, no . . . that's the particular dog that me and my friend we liked it, the pit bull.

Michelle: Where did you get him?

Alvin: Friends . . . in Riviera [Beach] it's like almost everybody owns one. . . . [but] I really don't care about, you know, really fighting them; it's just over there in Riviera Beach . . . there is a lot of people that have a lot of pit bulls in their backyards, like they build special cages for 'em, and I know a couple of people that sometime take dogs to dog fights. . . . They go all the way to Fort Lauderdale—like I guess they make a lot of money off of it also, you know what I'm saying?

Michelle: [What about the] training that they do, the big heavy chains that they have to wear around their necks in order for their necks to get strong . . .

Alvin: Yeah.

Michelle: And the things that they feed them, gunpowder, things like that that I've heard that they do.

Alvin: I heard that but I ain't actually ever seen anybody feeding the dog any gunpowder, I just heard about it.

Michelle: Hanging 'em from a tree by their jaws to make them strong.

Alvin: Yeah, my dog used to be tied up in the back yard, he'd just run around the back yard like when the wind blows and the tire goes circling around, he would just jump up there and bite on it and hang up there for like hours at a time on his own.

Michelle: On his own?

Alvin: Yeah.

Michelle: You don't think that's a little uncomfortable?

Alvin: I'm pretty sure it is uncomfortable, but you know, he lets go, he let go and run around and some of the wind started blowing and he'd run back up there and jump and grab on some more and just hang up there and—

Michelle: What about using other animals for baiting? Kittens?

Alvin: . . . There is this guy, he used to always have these big raccoon cages and he always used to go catch raccoons and . . . he used to fight the dogs with the raccoons . . . Some of the dogs got hurt fighting raccoons and some killed the raccoons. . . .

Michelle: What else do they use to train them?

Alvin: What they use to train them? Like they use another dog, or [something that is . . .] more of a challenge, like a raccoon or perhaps a bigger dog. . . .

Michelle: What happens when their dog loses?

Alvin: I know a lot of people that killed their dogs when the dog loses, like if the dogs happen to like scream during the fight or he put his tail between his leg, they call it a cur, I seen people kill their dog 'cause of that, just kill 'em right there on the spot and just leave them right there.

Michelle: They shoot them?

Alvin: They'd shoot them, hit them in the head with a hammer, you know what I'm saying, I seen it done before.

Michelle: . . . But when you are around an animal for a certain length of time, you have to have some kind of feeling for them and compassion for them.

Alvin: Right, right, me personally, I never put a dog like to fight . . . and had it killed. ..'cause it was like basically me and my friends just doing this, but I know these other people that . . . are deeply involved into it and basically they have like fifty dogs in their back yards, special made pens for all of them. . . . Like this guy that I know, he got this big old back yard, right, and he has puppy cages. . . . He got like fifteen little puppy pit bulls that he is raising on this site. And on this site, the male dogs fight, the female dogs, the pregnant dogs, know what I'm saying, everything is really organized. . . . And when they go bet on a fight, it's like . . . two thousand, five thousand dollars or better. They go somewhere like, know what I'm saying, they go a lot of different places, they'll go up north, Jacksonville, they go all the way up to Georgia. They'll take a dog all the way up to Georgia just to go fight.

Michelle: So it's highly organized?

Alvin: Yeah.

Michelle: So, obviously there is no way that we can appeal to these people to be more compassionate?

Alvin: So, its not even about being compassionate, it's more [about] sport and money, know what I'm saying, its not about being . . ."Oh, don't you care about the dog?" It's not about that.

Michelle: I mean, obviously these people aren't stupid, because they figured out how to run a business, so they must know that dogs have the same nervous system—exactly the same nervous system that we do, I mean, we are the same.

Alvin: Right.

Michelle:In terms of the cellular level we are all the same; I mean, we all have a liver, we all have a heart, we all have lungs, we reproduce the same. Everything is the same. So, they don't consider that they feel pain the same way we do?

Alvin: I guess they don't care, 'cause, know what I'm saying, in a way they care, *but they care about the money*, that's what this is all about, the money. I know this guy after he gets through fighting the dogs, if his dogs get cut he stitch the dog up himself. . . . He got all of everything, he orders everything. He got this big old magazine, this veterinary magazine where they sell all this stuff and he buy big old boxes of things at a time, like shots, everything. . . . like his own little doctor at the same time. He even cuts his own dogs' ears.

Michelle: With no anesthesia? How does that make you feel?

Alvin: It makes me feel kinda . . . I know it's wrong, I know it's hurting the dogs, 'cause one time I seen them cut this dog's ears, right, and he has this other kid, he was like, "Tape these two front paws up like this and tape the two back paws . . ." and he had this other guy like holding him down, holding the dog down like this, and then he had some tape, so he put it on the dog's ear, so, you know what I'm saying, so it's nice and even. And he'd take like some sharp scissors and he would cut the dog's ears and the dog is just, know what I'm saying, he fighting to get up but he can't, he shitting all over his self, know what I'm saying, I guess it's so painful . . . and he just cut the ear, they cut it and they fix it up and he get a needle and then he'll like tie the two tips of the ear so like it stays up after it heals and like in a week or two like a month later I seen the dog and, know what I'm saying, it look like it was professionally done, know what I'm saying, the way it looked and it healed up right, it was standing up straight, so I guess just the process of doing, that's where is really not good, cause I done seen the dog shit on itself, I'm talking about hollering. . . .

Michelle: An older dog?

Alvin: No, puppies, like maybe four months old, five months old, or maybe even less than that.

Michelle: Alvin, the reason the state of Florida takes such a hard stance against dog fighting and animal abuse in general is because people that hurt animals will go on and hurt people. We know this, it's proven. Jeff Dahmer, you know who he is?

Alvin: Right.

Michelle: He killed animals, he abused animals. The kids who killed all those students in Columbine were shooting neighborhood cats just the week before, but the police dismissed it as "boys will be boys."

Alvin: Right.

Michelle: And we know . . . that the people who abuse animals are going to go on to abuse people. So the reason they take it so seriously . . . is because they want to get you in the system and they want to watch you and they want to make sure that they know who you are, because they figure it's just a matter of time before you do something like that to a person. How do you feel about that?

Alvin: Guilty.

Michelle: Do you agree with that?

Alvin: Yes, I do agree with that.

Michelle: Do you think that there is anything that we can do to stop it? What about monetary rewards? The Humane Society is offering a $2,500 reward for every name you turn it that leads to the arrest of the dog fighter or to the rescue of a dog pit bull.

Alvin: I don't think it will really make a difference, but if they go to jail . . . it'll slow the process down a little bit, you know, 'cause some of the people I know . . . cars ride by their house every day and can't tell nothing, house look all right in the front yard, nice roses and everything, and the back yard is like battlegrounds, I guess.

Michelle: Why don't the neighbors turn them in?

Alvin: The neighbors? The neighbors really don't talk, some of the neighbors don't even know, like this dude I'm talking about you know he got in his back yard, he has like a hill, it's like a little mountain and he goes underground, know what I'm saying, that's where he fights the dogs at, after you close that door and you are underground you don't hear anything, you can go in there and shoot a gun and you won't hear anything.

Michelle: Is it a cultural thing, is it a black, white thing . . . ?

Alvin: I don't really think so, 'cause some of the dog fights that I've been to I see white folks from Palm Beach, know what I'm saying, pull up in the big Mercedes Benz . . . [and] there is a couple of guys . . . like some rednecks I guess you can say. . . . But when it come down to the money, everyone gets together, know what I'm saying, everyone has a couple of beers. . . . You can have people that don't have any dogs that just come to make the money, and then there is people that bring their own dog to fight, you know. . . . Cops are involved in it, too, so how can you say it's a racial thing?

Michelle: How widespread is this?

Alvin: How?

Michelle: How big is this?

Alvin: Real big, real, real big.

Michelle: Do they use other dogs, Rottweilers or Dobermans, shepherds, chow chows, anything like that?

Alvin: Just pit bulls.

Michelle: . . . And do they use [other dogs] for training?

Alvin: They use them for training too, but you know what I'm saying, when they go fight the dogs, they have like special rules . . . they fight a chow chow, 'cause the chow has too much hair, know what I'm saying so it would be a disadvantage, so they like weigh the dog. . . . The age really doesn't matter, just as long as they are the same size, that is what counts. They won't fight a German Shepard with a pit bull, 'cause they say the same thing, the hair. I know this guy from Miami, he had this pit bull, I'm talking about this dog used to always fight and was winning all these fights, it was one of his prize dogs, you know, and all the teeth of the dog were gone, all of them were gone. . . . He took the dog to Miami somewhere and got implants put in the dog's mouth. He paid over seven thousand dollars just for that. . . . He told me that he paid over seven thousand dollars; he showed me the dog's mouth. The dog had four fangs, an inch and a half long. I'm like damn, how he eat? He still had his lowers.

Michelle: And they never go to vets?

Alvin: No. They do their own. They have their own files, they keep track of when the shots are due. Sometimes they'll take like the stool, they'll take the stool to like a veterinarian place to get the stool examined, but they never take the dogs. Some of these people that been in the newspaper selling pit bull puppies, almost all are them, know what I'm saying? You might find a couple of them that's all right, that's selling them dogs cause they are trying to sell them, but most of them, they be breeding the dogs and fighting them and when they get them pregnant that's another way of making money, selling puppies for five, six hundred dollars.

Michelle: So you think the only way that we're going to be able to do anything about this is to set up some sort of a reward system?

Alvin: A reward system? Basically, yeah, that's about it. . . . If somebody think they gonna get paid for turning the person in, cause this person is doing something wrong, know what I'm saying, certain people are gonna be like all right . . . because it's all through the neighborhood, everybody doing it. Like on a holiday, like on a Fourth of July, you know what I'm saying, you see like big old parties and in the back yard they fighting dogs, know what I'm saying, everybody just drinking and watching the fight.

Michelle: And nobody ever, nobody in this huge group of people, thinks that it's wrong, or feels sorry, nobody feels sorry for the dogs?

Alvin: No, know what I'm saying, most of the people that be there, know what I'm saying, they already know what time it is. . . . A lot of dope dealers be there, know what I'm saying? Then again, you got rich white folks be there too, and everybody know what time it is, they already got their deposit in there. ..already put they money down, you know . . .

Michelle: Right.

Alvin: They not gonna lose no money like that. These things they be costing some money, I'm taking about like two, three, four, five thousand dollars just a bet, the fight might last thirty minutes, then again, it might go on for two, three hours.

Michelle: And when the dogs are hurt, they don't go to the vet, nobody takes care of their wounds, or do they just stich them up themselves?

Alvin: Yes.

Michelle: Don't they die from infections?

Alvin: No, I've never seen [that]. Maybe I've seen like one or two dogs die from the infection, but they take care of them pretty well, they heal up real quick. . . . [25] I've seen dogs like when they don't want to fight, the guy just come up with like a hammer and just hit real hard right across the head. And all you see is the dog just fall and die. . . . They dig a hole, some people they bury 'em and then again some people just throw 'em in a garbage bag and throw 'em in the dump, know what I'm saying?

Michelle: And the only way to get in there is to have a dog that you are bringing in to bet.

Alvin: Yeah, you either bringing in the dog and you bet, yep.

Alvin completed his community service by working for Dr. Berkenblit at Village Animal Clinic. During his time there, Alvin was responsible for bathing and walking dogs, mopping kennels and picking up around the grounds. I assigned several videos for him to watch and spoke with him after he did so. One of the videos was *Final Round*, available from the Humane Society of the United States (HSUS), a particularly graphic video of dog and cock fighting. The other video was *Dogs with Jobs*, a video that celebrates the services that some dogs perform for people as therapy dogs, search and rescue dogs, and dogs who can foretell seizures and cardiac arrest in humans. The latter video was shown to him in an effort to establish the wonderful qualities that dogs have. I hoped Alvin would learn that instead of abusing and killing dogs, we should find more ways to protect them. Alvin seemed impressed with the videos, and I hope he was sincere in his agreement with their message, but at the end of our interaction I felt I would not hear anything more about Alvin unless he got into trouble again—something I hope will never happen.

Several months after my interview with Alvin, a sheriff's deputy named Reginald Mickens, who had been arrested almost a year before, requested that he be allowed to perform his community service hours with our shelter. The shelter manager was not anxious to help the deputy discharge his responsibility, but since it was only forty hours (his only punishment aside for some "leave with pay"), he agreed to do so. Once more, I sat across the desk from a convicted dog fighter and asked some hard questions. This man was not nearly as forthcoming as the young Alvin, and he denied the charges.

Michelle: What were you doing at a dog fight? It's illegal and you're a cop!

Mickens: I didn't know it was a dog fight. I was told I was going to a barbeque.

Michelle: So when you got there, why didn't you call the cops?

Mickens: They walked in right behind me.

Michelle: So are you still fighting dogs?

Mickens: I ain't got no dogs. (This was a lie.)

Michelle: So how do you feel about dogfighting?

Mickens: I don't know nothing about it.

Michelle: So how are your fellow officers treating you since your arrest?

Mickens: They pre-judged me. They don't talk to me because they pre-judged without hearing my side.

Unfortunately, I could not force him to be honest with me, and I learned nothing from this interview. The moment Mickens left my office, I called the arresting officer on his case, Detective Cassie Kovacs, an extremely dedicated and professional officer on a personal mission to stop dog fighting or die trying. I told her what he had said. "The room was packed full of people and he was at the farthest side of the room," she told me. "He had to have been there for quite some time to be in the position he was in. It was standing room only and nobody else could enter the room."

Several days later I had occasion again to speak to Cassie. This time, a couple had come to our shelter with two pitiful pit bulls. They had come for their rabies tags and shots. The young man was full of braggadocio about his exploits with his "hog dog" and pit bulls. He talked loud and long to anyone who would listen about how he trained his dogs to hunt hogs, and how his pit bulls love to fight and never lost. And I was very willing to listen. As soon as they left, I obtained the address from the rabies form and called Cassie. Later that week, the sheriff's helicopter flew over the address and found a disturbing scene of a pit bull wearing a bulletproof vest while tearing apart a young pig who was very much alive. This was probable cause for a search warrant, and that case is now pending.

It is up to humane educators to take the lead in stopping blood sports in our communities. I recommend the *Final Round* video, which I show in middle- and high-school classes, though some elementary school teachers have requested it as well. It includes footage of dog and cock fighting as well as interviews with animal control officers with the Michigan Humane Society. Another excellent video is *One Last Fight, Exposing the Shame*, by John Caruso of the Anti-Cruelty Society of Chicago. John wanted to produce this film because he believes dog fighting is a detriment to the community and the neighborhood. "Animal activists, humane societies and rescue organizations have been yelling about animal cruelty from the rooftops for years," he says, "but our voices were never heard until the link between animal cruelty and family violence became clear. All of a sudden this little cocoon in which animal advocates were isolated and insulated for so long exploded, and now everyone understands the urgency of paying attention to animal cruelty. When there is dog fighting in the neighborhood, there are all these attendant crimes that go along with that. There are typically drugs, illegal weapons, gambling, assaults, even murder. And the little old lady who lives two houses down from where abused pit bulls are being held cannot even walk to her mailbox without fear of attack by a loose dog. Children are easy targets for dogs who break out of their bondage. The noise of pit bull fights is bad enough, but then music is turned up loud to drown out the screams of dogs in pain or the people cheering them on. Dog fighting does not just affect dogs. Oh, no, its reach is far and wide. And just think what it does to little kids who have to witness dog fighting."

Dr. MaryLou Randour, Director of Education for the Doris Day Animal Foundation and a member of Psychologists for the Ethical Treatment of Animals (PSYETA), believes that dog fighting is very damaging to children exposed to it. "They get used to violence and habituated to it in a way. For them it's about money but there is also suffering. They are not used to thinking about it from another perspective. I think it is hard for them to think about what anything is like from another person's perspective, and then to take it to the next step and think from an animal's perspective. In working with batterers the first thing you have to chip away at is getting someone to understand a situation from another person's perspective. You can start by doing it cognitively, where they can get an intellectual understanding, or you can do it through feeling—what does this feel like to the other person. But that is empathy training. You can't be empathic if you can't understand what it is like to be a dog or cat or whatever. They are thinking about money but forgetting that there is another perspective here."

MaryLou feels it is important when addressing students on the issue of dog fighting to teach them what perspective means. " 'Play a game with me,' " she demonstrates with an imaginary student. " 'You look very smart and I bet you can do this. You have to have a really good creative intelligence, but I think that you do, so why don't you imagine being a dog? You may need some information about being a dog,' " she continues, " 'so let me ask you this: Do you know that dogs feel pain?' and go on with feelings, facts. 'Now that you have these facts, tell me from the dog's point of view what does it feel like if this happens, if that happens.' See if they can do it. But you are going to have to help them by setting it up so they feel like they are doing something challenging. You are going to try to get them to increase their perspective so that they can have theirs plus another's perspective."

But humane educators must do more than just convince kids not to fight their dogs, says Kelley Filson of the San Francisco Society for the Prevention of Cruelty to Animals. "You can't replace something with nothing," she stresses. "You have to give them something to take the place of the activity you are taking away. I have been working for about the last two years with a young man who was engaged in pit bull fighting. This guy lives in the Hunters Bay Point district of San Francisco that is known as "the projects." My problems there primarily stem from dog fighting. The people who live there are very poor. It is also a violent place. The animal control officers will not go there without police officers escorting them. I drive into this area to teach classes because I think it is important to reach these kids. The thing this young man has most impressed upon me is that dog fighting really is about money. We just cannot fault them for that. The other stimulus is power. They have nothing in their lives, and a powerful dog that will keep them safe in their homes and be an external display of something valuable is a motivating force. They do love their dogs in their own way, even though we cannot comprehend that. And the younger they are, the more they love their dogs. But you cannot replace something with nothing. There needs to be an activity for them to do with their dogs. They need to win a competition, they need to get prize money and they need to have something to do."

It is a good idea to know about agility trials, obedience classes and other legal and beneficial forms of competition involving dogs. Having that information with you and encouraging students to try new things will go a long way toward cutting down on the animal fighting problems we see in our day-to-day lives.

Familiarize yourself with your state statutes as they relate to dog fighting and animal baiting, and make copies to share. See if a police officer will come along with you in a joint effort to teach kids to stay out of trouble by avoiding this ever-growing activity. Make up little cards that have a local phone number where kids can call with information. They may earn a reward offered by HSUS.

But of course, early intervention is a key element of humane education. We hope to enable the kids we visit in classrooms today—kids who are growing up in a world like Alvin's—to look at that world in a different way, and choose a different path. One way to awaken says Dr. Mary Lou Randour, is by engaging the children with stories. "If you can tell stories of some of the cruelty cases you are aware of, it does not hurt them psychologically, and in terms of capturing and keeping their attention, the grislier the better," she argues. Video games and television, she says, show kids images that are far worse than anything you can tell them. "Kids tend to tune in more when you tell them a story," she says, "And you can make points of discovery where instead of making a presentation to kids on the link between animal abuse and human violence and how it affects our psyche, you can ask questions about 'Have you ever seen this?' Or tell stories of some of the cases you have heard or seen. Then, engage them. Ask them what they think causes it and what kind of person does this, what effect will it have on the kids who do this? You can give them the information through a process of discussion rather than just lecturing. I think it is important to ask kids about this stuff."

I told Dr. Randour the story of Sadie, a little Pomeranian who had been hit by a car and left by the side of the road. The nature of her injuries was such that it appeared that she had been deliberately abused. The story isn't pretty, and the facts are very sad. But I tell the story to middle- and high-school kids because there is a lesson to be learned in the mistakes that we, the authorities, made in handling this case. I sense a palpable quickening in the energy in the room, a heightened sense of alertness. The students are suddenly paying attention to this "war story" and responding, getting involved. I was concerned that the story might be too graphic for these kids, too disturbing. But Dr. Randour convinced me that not only are these kids already subjected to violence, gore and cruelty, but the consequences to society if we continue to ignore animal cruelty are dire.

There is reason for hope in the story of Lavon, a little boy who has stolen my heart. He's a tiny boy, very slight. I meet with Lavon and his classmates every Friday morning at 10:00 in their classroom. Woody and Katie have fallen head over tail for this child as well. At first, Lavon was very angry. He certainly didn't want to get involved with humane education. He bragged all about his uncles and their fighting pit bulls. He wanted me to understand that his uncles' dogs were all purebred pit bulls, because, as he stated, he absolutely hated mutts and felt they should all be killed. I told him, "But I am a mutt! I am a mixture of Irish and Norwegian; that makes me a mixed breed, a mutt!" (He conceded that I shouldn't be killed for not being of pure descent.)

Lavon relished my discomfort as he related stories about dogs who lost fights and were left to die in abandoned fields. This was a child who was the very personification of anger.

How then did I, a middle-aged white lady from New York, relate to this angry young street-wise African-American kid from the South?

Lavon's intelligence appealed to me. He was certainly the leader in this little class of misfits, a group of children whom, at the tender age of eight, nine or ten, society had pretty much given up on. This was a class that would have been called "alternative education" or, more aptly, "drop-out prevention" in the more senior grades—but this was elementary school. These kids had not even made it to third grade yet, and already they had done something so heinous as to get them expelled, suspended or even arrested.

Vanessa Reeves is the behavior intervention specialist in Lavon's class. There are several of these highly specialized disciplinarians who assist the teacher in keeping order in the classrooms. As she describes it, some of these kids have such horrendous home lives, with nobody who really cares for them, or gives them the time of day, that it is a wonder they even survive. "They can look at you and see something from their past, something that just goes click in their minds, and before you know it, they attack you for no reason. They can be very dangerous kids. But [humane education] is a great program for kids like this. I wish there were a hundred 'Ms. Michelles' to go around! Every kid needs this; every kid needs to learn respect for the world around them. This is a great way to do it, and it shows these kids that people still care about them. Someone still thinks they are worth teaching, taking time with, getting to know. This program is therapeutic as well as educational. It helps the kids to see how other people see the world—how animals are important to so many people and for so many reasons. They surely are not getting this message at home."

One of my favorite lessons with this class and other classes like it is to read the book *If You Give a Mouse a Cookie* and to use the teacher workbook that goes along with this wonderful story. The book, one of many in a series written by Laura Numeroff and beautifully illustrated by Felicia Bond, lends itself to humane education in so many ways. The teachers appreciate the critical thinking and logic skills inherent in the books ("if you do *this*, than *that* will happen"). The kids appreciate the pretty pictures and the whimsical story line. Humane educators appreciate that the story is about pleasing a mouse, one of the smallest of earth's creatures, and one that people destroy in the most inhumane ways.

When there are just a few kids in the class or group, it's easy to involve everyone. I have hand puppets that I pass out to the kids and they take turns reading the book using the mouse or human puppet to read the lines. Lavon loves to play the part of the mouse, and he has taken to paraphrasing the lines. For example, he will read "If you give a mouse a cookie" as written, then make the mouse puppet say, "Yo, lay a cookie on me, bro." The kids in the class are delighted at the creativity and they all follow suit, each coming up with something more original and witty than the last. Before you know it, we have an improvised, interactive comedy skit with no place for anger, depression or resentment.

In classrooms across the country, humane educators are working to counteract disrespect and cruelty to animals with activities like these. As in the old Cherokee's story, we do our best to feed a child's capacity for love and kindness, compassion and faith, to give that "wolf"—and the domesticated wolves who share our lives—a fighting chance.

13

Psychologically Speaking

NATHANIEL BRAZIL WAS MAD at his favorite teacher, Mr. Grunow, because he wouldn't let him say goodbye to his girlfriend during class time. So he took a gun and shot Barry Grunow dead. Nate Brazil, at the tender age of fourteen, was convicted as an adult and is serving twenty-eight years in Florida's prison system. Mr. Grunow's widow and children are left alone in the world, cheated of the life they would have had with her husband, their father. Nathanial Brazil was reputed to be a happy, funny, popular kid. So why was he so angry?

More and more children are exhibiting the signs and symptoms of anger, and school systems are employing non-educators such as behavior management specialists, social service workers and the like to deal with so called "problem" students. This is one of the reasons why the need and demand for humane educators is so high. The door is wide open to those who would accept the challenge to work with the children others have given up on. When all else fails, bring in the dogs!

Dr. MaryLou Randour, Director of Education for the Doris Day Animal Foundation, does not believe that all crimes committed by children are born out of anger. Just as there is diversity among kids, she says, there is diversity in their reasons for doing the things that they do. "I don't think that all kids are angry," she says. "I think we need to have an open mind and consider that kids commit crimes against animals for a variety of reasons that may have nothing to do with anger. I think we need to first find out why a kid does what he does and then find a remedy that works to bring about a change in their attitudes and behaviors. I am very interested in how we should treat animal abuse now that the general public is more aware of its importance in the scheme of things. Now that there are some convictions or even just investigations, what do you do with a juvenile or an adult? What psychological treatments should we use?

"But more importantly, we should not wait until a kid gets in trouble. There are ways to teach empathy development and to teach about the animal–human bond and the importance of human–animal interactions. PSYETA and the Doris Day Animal Foundation have developed Anicare, a joint project that offers a comprehensive approach for treating animal abuse. It's a tool that can be used by experienced therapists to interrupt the cycle of violence. But some of the exercises Anicare offers can be used in the classroom."

Dr. Randour admits that experts really don't know what therapies work for treating those who abuse animals, because nobody has really studied the question. Only relatively recently has society come to accept that animal abuse is a serious issue that should not be taken lightly. Because of this lack of attention, there is a lack of information on what kind of therapeutic or prevention intervention is most effective. And, she says, we have to be very careful not to aggravate the problem. "I remember when I started reviewing the literature from the American Psychological Association on violence programs in general," Dr. Randour remarks. "Some of the violence reduction programs that were offered to a variety of schools and school systems were evaluated and found to actually increase violence! So we now know that just because just because you have an intervention does not mean it's going to work. But the problem is, as with everything else, it's very costly to do really good research. So what we ended up doing in Anicare Child is work by analogy. I reviewed the research of the kinds of interventions that are effective with kids that have conduct disorders. The thinking is that a lot of the kids that are abusing animals would fall into that category. Then, we adapted those approaches to the approach we used in Anicare Child. One of the things we lack is good information on what does work and finding ways to track your intervention to see what effect it's had on the teachers that have received it."

An additional challenge lies in the fact that humane educators are not like therapists who see a patient week after week. At best, we see students on an occasional basis, and sometimes we only get to see them once in a group setting. Since we have a limited time with a child or group of children, how can we best use that time? What is the main message we want the children to remember?

Dr. Randour suggests, "I think we need to identify reporting animal cruelty as a public health issue. That would be my goal. Treat animal abuse as a public health issue so that kids are trained just like they are trained to report emergencies to 911 if there is a fire or some other emergency. Make sure that they understand the importance of reporting if they hear or know about animal cruelty. Juveniles frequently know about it before anyone else. Teach them why it is important—that a creature is being hurt, but also that kids who do that are in trouble in some way. They are learning some behaviors that are going to harm them in some way developmentally. Naturally, we need to put it in a language kids understand. Explain to them that getting away with violence towards animals gets them used to behaving violently so they are more inclined to operate that way when they are a parent or a spouse. It just hardens them in some way. So if they are reported, they can get help."

Dr. Randour believes that some kids who do perpetuate cruelty to animals may become serial killers or school shooters, but a lot of them are just becoming regular citizens who are very rough with their wife and children. We never hear of those cases. The families and the animals involved suffer in silence. "It's a continuum of effect from the most extreme—the serial killers and the school shooters—to these kind of everyday citizens who have become callous in some way and used to using interpersonal violence to negotiate a relationship and may never make it to a police blotter anywhere," she says.

"So that is why I think it is important for kids to pay attention to this and how they can help society, help the animals, and help the kids who are doing it. We need to be giving them resources and procedures and processes to follow. It's not that complicated.

"I think it would be great for the humane educators to

facilitate discussions with kids. Ask them, have you ever seen someone abusing an animal? What did you do about it? What could you do about it if you heard this? What if you are walking home from school and you saw some kids and you knew that they were doing something bad to an animal? What would you do? What could you do? And it's a good idea to let the class know that you have heard about this before, maybe even from other classes. You could begin by saying that you went to this other school and this is what the kids told me, or has this ever happened to you? Have you ever heard of this?

"Teach them what to do. Educators should know their local laws, numbers to call, agencies that will help. Then, like a fire drill, the kids will be better prepared to know what to do because they have rehearsed it. Have a number of hypothetical situations ready and ask them, What would you do if this occurred, what about this? What are the possibilities? What if the guys were bullying you? What if you reported it to your teacher and the teacher didn't do anything? Who else could you tell? What are some other possibilities? What may happen once you do report it?"

I guess it is no revelation that most people would prefer to join in a discussion or conversation than simply be lectured to. Humane educators who simply give presentations may be getting the message out, but interaction with the class is truly better than lecturing and giving them thirty seconds at the end of the lesson for "any questions" they may have. Dr. Randour explains that our brains are wired in such a way that we learn much more when a point is made through storytelling than through lecturing. Stories, or narratives, are especially effective for teaching values. Jesus knew this and spoke in parables. Buddha, too, spoke in parables. The bible is full of allegories and anecdotes. Stories provide the framework, the perspective, the environment—and, since they can be true, they reflect our life experiences. Stories can dramatize abstract ideas in a way that captures and retains our attention. They also create understanding, sympathy and compassion. We feel for the characters, identify with them and make judgments on whether they behaved properly. Stories allow us to prepare and train for situations we may one day face ourselves. Telling stories to kids in class, evoking discussion and summarizing ideas and concepts is a far better way of teaching empathy than lectures or handouts.

And teaching empathy is a very important, if not the most important lesson that you can teach kids, says Dr. Randour. "If you can, tell stories of some of the cruelty cases you are aware of. It does not hurt them psychologically, and in terms of capturing and keeping their attention, the grislier the better." Video games and television, she says, show kids images that are far worse than anything you can tell them. "Kids tend to tune in more when you tell them a story," she says, "and you can make points of discovery where instead of making a presentation to kids on the link between animal abuse and human violence and how it affects our psyche, you can ask them, 'Have you ever seen this?' Or tell stories of some of the cases you have heard or seen. Then, engage them. Ask them what they think causes it and what kind of person does this, what effect it will have on the kids who do this. You can give them the information through a process of discussion rather than just lecturing. I think it is important to ask kids about this stuff."

I told Dr. Randour the story of Sadie, a little Pomeranian who had been hit by a car and left by the side of the road. The nature of her injuries was such that it appeared that she had been deliberately abused. The story isn't pretty and the facts are very sad. But I tell the story to middle and high school kids because there is a lesson to be learned in the mistakes that we, the authorities, handled this case. And when I do, I see a palpable quickening in the energy in the room, a heightened sense of alertness. The students are suddenly paying attention to this "war story" and responding, getting involved. I was concerned that this story may be too graphic for these kids, too disturbing. But Dr. Randour convinced me not only that these kids are already subjected to violence, gore and cruelty, but that the consequences to society if we continue to ignore animal cruelty are dire.

Another effective technique is combining storytelling with role playing. We can teach empathy development through learning about another's perspective. The ability to take on the role of another creature, to experience more than one perspective, is a cognitive developmental skill that some kids don't have. However, most kids can learn it. Dr. Randour advises, "Tell them stories that they can relate to for one reason or another . . . [then] let them talk. If a story is gruesome you can still tell it if there is an alternative response that they can come up with if they had been present. I think that the idea that they could have come to the aid of somebody should be your rule not whether it is uplifting or shocking." Tell the story of an animal victim, and then ask students to step into the role of the animal, the abuser, a witness or even the person who loves the animal and now has to deal with his or her injuries. While we can't always step into the shoes of those we seek to understand, we can try to do the next best thing—to see the world through the eyes of a frog, a mouse, a cat or a cow being led to slaughter.

I wondered if empathy could truly be taught or if it was

innate and therefore a kind of "got it or ain't got it" personality trait. I know, for example, that most of the hard-core animal-rights activists I know feel a deep and abiding, unequivocal empathy for the suffering of all animals that the garden-variety "animal lover" does not feel. Can someone truly be taught to empathize with a species other than their own? I put this question to Steve Best, Associate Professor of Philosophy and Humanities and Chair of Philosophy at the University of Texas, El Paso. "The answer to this question depends upon one's theory of 'human nature,' he began. "Competing interpretations oscillate between pessimistic views of human beings as violent predators, inherently aggressive, and utopian views of human beings as inherently good, but corrupted by society (e.g., Rousseau[26]). History suggests that human beings display a full range of behaviors, traits and potentialities, ranging from murder to love. If we adopt the rosy view of human nature, then humans are naturally empathetic and empathy should not need to be taught. If empathy is lost, it needs to be recovered as a vital and natural instinct of human beings—as David Hume correctly suggests that all ethics begins with the immediate empathetic identification with the suffering of another.[27] This means that the lack of empathy needs to be *unlearned* in order to recover the moral core of the human that is part of our evolutionary heritage. If we believe, however, that human beings are more prone to aggression and violence, then empathy is something that needs to be taught, and, if human nature is sufficiently flexible, empathy can be taught. If humans are so morally degraded that alienation is more present to them than identification, then empathy indeed must be taught. The very question of whether or not empathy can be taught thus is symptomatic of a society where morals are in question, for empathy should be part of the constitution of a healthy species."

But who, exactly, is in the best position to teach empathy? In an inner-city school where most of the students are African-American, Haitian or Hispanic, and most of the humane societies are made up of white, middle-class volunteers and humane educators, how do we make our point? Dr. Best answers: "People of color are suspicious of white concerns for animals and the environment because they see these as values of the privileged classes who, from their base of material comfort, orient their moral compass toward the natural world rather than the social world, and thus demonstrate elitist views. There is some historical basis for this belief in the history of the environmental and animal rights movements. For instance, the Sierra Club barred blacks and Jews from membership until the late 1950s. Educators have to be keenly aware of the distrust poor people and people of color often have toward environmentalism and animal rights. The dualist attitude of "us vs. them" has to be broken down so that it is clear that animal abuse has a negative impact on all human beings, regardless of race, class, or gender.

"Children from impoverished families may be tougher to convince because they are by necessity more focused on their own immediate needs. Concern for others of any species becomes a more distant and abstract concern. Often, one's moral circle is expanded to the degree one's own needs are satisfied. [These children] are not impossible to reach, however. We can still teach them by demonstrating the connections between the welfare of animals and the welfare of human beings, and, ideally, by helping them to see that compassion for others of any kind is spiritually uplifting for the self. If their empathetic nature is intact, they will not want their suffering to perpetuate that of another being. Remind them that there are profound connections between oppressed animals and oppressed human beings, and explain that everyone, regardless of class or ethnic background has responsibilities to animals and can evolve morally and spiritually by caring for them—this does not cost money."

Here again, we see the importance of teaching character education and empathy before we can teach other ideals. And teach it we must, as the following study shows.

South Carolina sociologist Clifton P. Flynn conducted a survey in which college students were asked if they had ever been cruel to animals as a child. The survey also asked the students' opinions on specific types of family violence. Forty-nine percent of the respondents had experienced animal cruelty in some way (either committing or witnessing it), and eighteen percent of the respondents had actually perpetrated the abuse. Males were much more likely than females to have been exposed to animal abuse, and were nearly four times more likely than females to have abused an animal. Flynn also noted that "respondents who had abused an animal were more likely to approve of a husband slapping his wife than those who had never committed animal abuse by three to one," and that "males who committed abuse against animals were spanked significantly more often by their fathers than those who had not committed animal cruelty." (He adds, "Frequency of spanking by mothers was not related to sons' animal cruelty.")[28]

In his article "Why Family Professionals Can No Longer Ignore Violence Toward Animals"[29] Flynn wrote that violence to animals has been largely ignored because society tends to value animal lives less than human lives and therefore violence or abuse towards animals is not taken seriously. He cited a study of the prosecution of animal cruelty cases in Massachusetts from 1975 to 1990 where less than half of the cases resulted in a conviction, and only one-third of those found guilty were fined. Even less, ten percent, were jailed. Since other issues are deemed more important, research dollars are not spent on animal cruelty issues, and grant money is not as available as it is for issues involving crimes against humans. The media is slow to cover animal cruelty cases, so the public is left with the perception that animal cruelty is rare. The study declares that a mere five percent of the 268 prosecuted cases of animal abuse were reported in the press. So crimes against animals are seen as isolated incidents and not as they truly are, connected and interwoven with crimes against people.

In addition to all those reasons, Flynn asserts that "the extensive amount of socially acceptable forms of violence against animals (i.e., hunting and fishing, animal experimentation, meat eating) are likely to contribute to an indifference about less acceptable forms of violence. When this cultural acceptance of the exploitation of animals is supported by powerful institutions of religion, science and government, and when those who are interested in the welfare of animals are perceived as overly emotional or irrational, then it is no surprise that so few social scientists have examined this phenomenon, particularly from a family perspective. Finally, animals, along with nonverbal human infants, are the only victims of systematic discrimination and exploitation who truly cannot speak on their own behalf. This silence makes it easier for all of us, including family professionals, to ignore their plight and its relation to our lives." Flynn argues that violence to animals must receive attention because it is a ". . . disturbing, antisocial and illegal behavior . . . that is most likely to lead to other forms of violence."

Linda Jo Fields Horse of the Winnebago Tribe in Nebraska related a story that had a chilling but illustrative effect. "We had a case where I knew the child was being abused. The child was hanging cats, kittens, puppies and rabbits, and progressed to beheading them. And when we found out we called law enforcement. Nobody really listened when we complained about the animal abuse, but I kept pushing it through child protective services. The child had burn marks and a lot of scarring on his back and his legs. He was showing us that he wanted help. This was the classic cry for help. I am the lone voice trying to educate all these agencies, police, tribal courts, social services, everyone, trying to educate them about the link between animal cruelty and domestic violence so that they will take animal cruelty and family violence more seriously. Native Americans are very private. They have the attitude that 'This is my problem, I will deal with it.' They don't air their problems. I want them to understand what the animals are there for."

Albert Schweitzer, the famous Nobel Prize winner, believed that "Very little of the great cruelty shown by men can really be attributed to cruel instinct. Most of it comes from thoughtlessness or inherited habit. The roots of cruelty, therefore, are not so much strong as widespread. But the time must come when inhumanity protected by custom and thoughtlessness will succumb before humanity championed by thought. Let us work that this time may come." And to that, we as humane educators say, "Amen!"

14

The Character Connection

"I am sometimes asked, 'Why do you spend so much of your time and money in talking about kindness to animals, when there is so much cruelty to men?' And I answer, 'I am working at the roots.' "

—George Angell, Founder Mass. SPCA

Character counts! This is the mantra that has been chanted over the past several years by school administrators and officials who are coming to the conclusion that reading, writing and arithmetic are no longer sufficient to raise responsible and trustworthy future leaders of our society.

The six pillars of character are trustworthiness, respect, responsibility, fairness, caring, and citizenship. These are certainly the qualities that parents and teachers want to instill in young minds. They also, coincidentally, describe the same behaviors we like to see people using when interacting with their animals.

Trustworthiness
You can trust me to feed you and meet your needs.

Respect
I respect you as a dog/cat/snake/hamster. . . .

Responsibility
I will keep you safe.

Fairness
I will make sure I understand you.

Caring
I will make sure you are healthy and comfortable.

Citizenship
I will do what the laws say
I should do to keep you well and safe
and insure you are not offending others

It is important to us as animal advocates for people to be responsible in meeting the needs of the animals in their care. It is vital that the people who count animals among their family members be good citizens and not let their animals run loose or hurt other animals, so that unnecessary laws are not passed prohibiting animals. Critical, too, is retention of companion animals in their families so that they are not turned in to shelters and needlessly euthanized. Therefore we hope that animals are well trained and that every effort is made to understand them so they are not surrendered at the first hint of trouble. Children should be raised to follow the example of parents and others who are fair in their dealings with veterinarians, animal-control officers and others, and fair in their judgment of animals who sometimes need extra help understanding what is expected of them. For us to accomplish these goals, we must recognize the connection between character education and humane education.

Most school systems have a character education program in place. Finding the people who are in charge of the character education in your school district will be your first step in merging humane education lessons with character education. These professionals will be happy to help you gain access to their students because you have so much to offer them. Teaching children to treat animals with respect and kindness is a basic concept that fits well into character education goals and objectives. As Bernard Orestes Unti wrote, "Wanton acts of individual cruelty against animal pets have come to be seen as the signs of a maladapted and sick personality. Conversely, a kind disposition toward such animals is considered an important attribute of the well-adjusted individual."[30] Teaching kindness is the job of both the character education teacher as well as humane educators, parents and other role models.

Kay Heisler, the Character Education Teacher for Lake Park Elementary School, explained to me why she called in a humane educator to help her reach her goals of instilling character in elementary-school age kids. Teaching character education to elementary-school children was a calling that Ms. Heisler answered with the blessing of a very progressive principal. It was a guidance counselor who first introduced Kay to an educator for a local domestic violence agency, AVDA (Aid to Victims of Domestic Abuse), who visited schools to teach lessons on family violence. "In watching her teach and listening and talking with her," says Kay, "she made me realize that people who commit violent crimes have grown up watching them being committed, and that there is a cycle that they go through. I learned that usually before they commit to a human, they have practiced on animals!" In learning this, Kay was committed to finding a way to break that well-known cycle. It is heartening that her first induction into the link between animal cruelty and violence to people was through a domestic violence agency and not an animal-oriented one. It means we are not alone out there!

Kay believes that humane education is needed because many schoolchildren are not being taught empathy for animals at home. "But having someone like you, a humane educator, come into the classroom is so important because through humane education they learn to become more sensitive. They buy in through character education. My lessons help to open the door and lay the foundation. Now you (the humane educator) are coming in and teaching them, repeating what I am saying yet illustrating how it pertains to animals, and they can relate it to these feelings that are being introduced to them."

But what about the messages that children are getting at home, which may be just the opposite of the lessons taught in character education or humane education? Kay says, "I still think that children trust, very much, those people who work with them in school as being people who are teaching them the right thing. And they may find themselves in the presence of other thoughts that contradict what we teach them, but they are now holding on to something that they will weigh out as being the better thing, the right thing. What I am looking forward to is the building we are doing, because the young ones are so open; they are not as resistant. And we build on that. Some of these kids now have had you come in two years in a row. Hopefully, the groundwork for sensitivity and caring would have been established and now it is just growing.

"The word empathy was never in their vocabulary, not even in their being. This is partly because they have had to be so tough to survive. So we are teaching them a different way. And especially the inner-city kids. There is more of a critical need for humane education in these schools. My assumption is that the ones that are coming from good homes do get the message at home. They have nice cats and dogs. They care for them. They see their parents take them to the vet when needed, include them in holidays, and generally treat them well. But I know that as far as the demographics is concerned with regard to character education, it is needed in all places. It is needed in schools where the kids come from great homes and it is needed in schools where the kids come from not-so-great homes. Look at the kids in Columbine! They came from good homes and privileged families and yet they killed cats and then people. Now when we think about treatment and care of the animals, I would say those in harsher home environments would need it more.

"Where upper-middle class families are concerned I would say that you do have some insensitivity, but it is on different levels, different ways. If there is someone shooting squirrels on their family estate, which of course is insensitive and cruel—but these folks are not involved in dog fighting and they probably spay and neuter their own animals, caring deeply for their own dogs and cats. Shooting wildlife is a terrible thing, but they get the message that caring for their own animals is good. So there is a degree of balance.

"In disadvantaged families, however, in the poorer neighborhoods, the standard is to see dogs not taken care of, having litter after litter after litter. So the bottom line is, I think they all need it. Some kids may need it in different ways. I think they all need to learn that the animal can't speak for him or herself, that this is a being that needs care. I think for my kids that has hit them more than anything. We ask them, 'What would your dog or cat say about you if he or she could talk? Would they say that this person takes care of me? He loves me? He understands me?'

"Maybe through teaching our kids about respect for animals we can become a kinder race even though we don't always agree on everything. But we can always talk and mediate. That is what we teach them in our character education classes, to choose the word over the fist. As far as humane education, they learn to care for the animals, and this will gradually phase out the insensitivity and uncaring and hurting of these animals, or even the indifference that makes them turn their heads the other way. We Americans find it so easy to turn the other way and not get involved and we have just got to come back to caring. That is my hope," says Kay.

A group called Peaceful Schools International awards a Peace Flag to certain schools that meet their criteria. "Can you imagine a day when every school has a peace flag?" muses Kay. "Some people say it would never happen, but Gandhi believed, 'We must be the change we wish to see.' I think people get tired and give up, but with the seeds we are planting in the young people now, they will have the strength, and the numbers, to make the difference we want to see."

I asked Kay to think about the children who are exposed to animal cruelty at home, and how they might respond to character and humane education. "In the instance of kids who are exposed to horrible animal cruelty, like dog fighting, we are dealing with cultural or familial influences," Kay began. "If the child is present when the actual hurting is taking place, and they see any of that, I believe they will remember the seed that we planted. Of course they may love that family member who is doing the hurting. But when they actually see it happening and they reflect back to what we taught them and they see the hurt, they will *get it*. They are going to still love their family member or friend, but they will realize that it is not right. They have probably seen that person do other things that have either scared them or made them angry, so the love would still be there, but now the validity of what is right makes them realize that maybe that person is making a bad choice. In character education we teach them that we have freedoms to make choices. We hear that in school all the time: "Billy, that is not a good choice." They are taught that with choices come consequences. Bad choices bring negative consequences, good choices bring positive consequences. So if they keep hearing this, and knowing that they have that freedom to choose, then they start to become more self-responsible.

"There is a song by Primary Focus that says 'If it is to be it's up to me!' Now I know that is putting a lot of responsibility on the child, and expecting a lot from the child, but in a child's realm, and their choices for the day, it very much fits, and as they get older their choices carry more weight but they are still their choices and the consequences thereof. . . . And the consequences of dog fighting are that you will end up with a torn-up dog or even a dead dog, and possibly a felony conviction. Those are choices that could be life altering. Even when they see people getting away with it all the time. It is an opportunity to teach them about cheating. The people who are involved in animal cruelty may be getting away with it, but those people are cheating. I like to tell a story about a med student who has cheated his whole way through med school. He cheated every step of the way and now he is practicing medicine. I ask my class "How would you like to go to him if you get sick?" He got away with it, but how does that affect us? Remember the sniper in the Baltimore area? I ask them to think of the families that are missing a family member now and explain how they are now cheated out of that family member."

Kay believes that character education is a movement, just like any other social movement. "I think we woke up as a nation one day and realized that we were not raising such nice people. And I think it dawned on us that rather than rehabilitate the ones that grow up to be troublesome adults, we should be working on raising more humane and empathetic children so that they will grow up to be better adults. So I see it as a movement and I think as with any movement it will catch on and get bigger. The Peaceful Schools International effort is a barometer for how well the movement is doing. How many schools were presented with the flag this year compared to last year?" I know that this is true of the animal-rights movement, where we look at fur sales, the stocks of companies still testing on animals, or the percentage of vegetarians as compared to a decade ago. This is what we look to as a barometer.

But Kay cautions, "I don't think we will know until twenty years from now how well character or humane education has done to stop the violence. We will have to look at who is getting arrested and why. I hope that this movement turns things around. The kids need to hear about the web of life, about how everything we do affects other things. When we preach how you have to love everybody and how everybody is your friend, it isn't going to work because it is not how it really is. You cannot expect the kids to like everyone. We don't like everyone. Can we expect and demand that they respect everyone? We can. They expect to be told that they have to always love their animals. But then you as the humane educator come in to tell them that they don't always have to love animals but they do have to respect them. You say, "It is not about loving animals, it's about respect." And maybe they don't always understand that right away, but they need to hear that. And they seem to buy into the fact, to allow the fact that they don't have to like everybody but they must respect them. I can see that your humane education lessons are working because I am hearing it back from the kids now."

15

Collaborations

"In order to educate the community, you have to get out into the community."

Wayne Pacelle, Co-Founder, Humane USA, Vice-President of Government Affairs, HSUS

"Animal people" frequently shy away from mainstream organizations and causes. Sometimes we do this because we have been made to feel unwelcome or have been criticized for our "radical" views and "fringe element" thinking. Consequently, activists tend to preach to the choir. But there is a better way to bring about change in our communities. Our communities, where people of influence and resolve gather, can become our classrooms. The best way for us to be a strong and powerful voice for the animals is to take part in our own communities at home. As the environmentalists in the '70s used to say, "Think globally, act locally." This slogan is applicable today, as animal welfare, animal rights and animal control people try to come together for the benefit of the animals. We can make some very important strides in our own communities where the rights of animals are concerned. Here are some ideas to get you started.

Now that we know that animal cruelty can sometimes lead to violence against humans, we can assume that we have allies in the domestic violence sector. Look for your local domestic violence advocates and join a council or committee such as Children and Family Services—an excellent starting point for teaching that animals are part of the family. We hear that said quite often, but do we really think about what it means? What does it mean, for instance, when the family has to evacuate because of flooding or a hurricane, and the animal is left behind? What does it mean when there is a divorce in the family, and the children are given over to one parent or the other, but the animal is sent to a shelter? Your presence at these domestic violence awareness gatherings assures that the animals will always be part of the consciousness of the group when they are coming up with new literature, posters or campaigns to raise awareness about domestic violence or legislative issues. For example, if they start adding questions to their intake forms such as "Is your dog being beaten?" along with "Are you being beaten?" it helps us to raise awareness of the importance of animals as part of the family. Or consider that more and more local humane societies have found that domestic violence victims often need someone to care for their animals so that they can go into a shelter. But if those domestic violence victims do not know that such care is available, they won't make that all-important first phone call to the hotline. This is where membership in committees to raise awareness becomes very important.

This does take time and effort on your part—you have to attend these meetings, build alliances, foster relationships and cultivate friendships within these councils—but the benefit to the animals is well worth it. You can't just make an irate phone call, out of the blue, to a domestic violence organization and demand to know why they are not taking care of animals as part of their mission statement. It just doesn't work that way. However, if you are part of the committee, part of the group, part of the solution, your credibility is raised and others will listen to you. They will also be more inclined to put you in touch with all the right people—judges, politicians and journalists—who may even be members themselves.

Does your county have an evacuation plan or hold regularly scheduled emergency procedures seminars? Try to get on a list of people who are notified and invited to these workshops and meetings. You can do this by signing up with your local public health agency or Red Cross chapter. If you attend these workshops, practices and exercises, you can be a voice for the animals. When your emergency officials are discussing natural, chemical or biological disaster preparedness, you can pipe up and say, "Do you have veterinarians on staff that can assist with injured animals?" You can start a discussion for the animals so that they are not left behind. If your local Red Cross does not allow animals at their shelters, find a shelter where they can go and help educate the community about acceptable Red Cross animal shelters in the event of a hurricane, tornado or flood. If you are thinking "But I work during the day," consider asking your employer about going as a designated employee from your company. For the cost of your hourly wage, your company can become members of a vitally important community organization.

Also consider teaching night classes. Many community schools offer night classes in everything from yoga to martial arts to foreign languages. Maybe you can offer to teach a vegetarian cooking class and earn a little money on the side. Vegetarian cooking is not only healthy, but it is good for the planet and the animals. Teaching a veg cooking class is a great way to be of service to animals in your community and to gain new friends and advocates. Or find an animal expert and ask him or her to offer problem-solving classes for people who tie up their dogs outside, rub their noses in their mistakes or otherwise mishandle common behavior problems. If you help someone get a class like that started, you will be educating a group that sorely needs it, and their companion animals will be forever grateful.

Start a local chapter of a vegetarian society or animal-advocacy group. If you get in touch with the Humane Activist Network of the Humane Society of the United States (HSUS), or People for the Ethical Treatment of Animals (PETA), they will send you a list of activists in your area who have given permission to be contacted. Set a meeting time and place, send out an email to all the local activists, and see who shows up! There is power in numbers. Or get involved with your local humane society in a variety of other ways. Take a shelter dog for a walk or to the local PetSmart on a Saturday afternoon so that he or she can get adopted. This is a rewarding experience for you and a life-altering experience for a lonely canine or feline who is counting down the days until someone comes along and places a big black X on his or her cage card.

Maybe you could offer to organize a fundraiser for your local shelter or rescue group. Don't just call them with great ideas for fundraisers (they really hate when people do that), but actually put one on for them. It's fun and easy and will bring you into contact with lots of other animal people so that you can form alliances and build support groups. That way, when you have the Great American Meatout or International Society for Animal Rights Homeless Animals Vigil in your hometown, you will already have a mailing list! A fundraiser can be anything from throwing a party and charging a fee to organizing a rummage sale, bake sale, CPR class or car wash. The money raised could be earmarked for spay/neuter efforts, humane education or a fund for animals needing medical care. Here's a sample press release:

Press Release

For Immediate Release
Contact: CallMe First at (xxx) xxx-xxxx

Humane Town, February 14

Pet First Aid and CPR Class Set for February 28

The Humane Town Humane Society is offering a pet CPR and first aid class from 7:00 to 8:00 P.M. on February 28 at 1 Humane Circle, Humane Town.

The class is taught by Dr. I. M. Cool, D.V.M., Humane Society Veterinarian, and will include important information on household dangers, the Heimlich maneuver for companion animals, first aid and related information. The class is free and open to the public, but donations are accepted. Reservations are not necessary. Please do not bring companion animals. Cookies and lemonade will be served. For information call xxx-xxxx.

Obtain the fax numbers or e-mail addresses of your local press and send it out about two weeks ahead of time. By the way, if you need help finding an instructor for a class like this one, you may wish to contact your local fire department. Most large fire departments have community educators who are available to teach fire safety and CPR, and animal mannequins are available to demonstrate CPR on dogs and cats.

Find the local breed rescue groups in your state and offer to help with fostering, transport or adoption. Breed rescue groups are usually comprised of dog breeders, so there may be differences of opinion among those who are working toward a no-kill nation; but again, concentrate on the common ground. Some people want certain breeds, and no matter how much we educate people as to the value and wonder of mixed-breed dogs, only a purebred will do. We don't want to send prospective dog adopters to irresponsible breeders, and we certainly don't want to send them to pet stores. Of course, a shelter can be a good place to find a purebred, because about one third of shelter dogs are purebreds. Breed-specific rescue is another viable alternative and one that we can all live with. We like breed rescue groups because they keep people out of pet stores, and that helps cut down on the puppy mill profits.[31] And if you are the local "animal person" and people are always asking you where they can get a specific breed, it will be helpful if you know ahead of time who in your community is working with breed rescue.

There are national organizations that need your help too.

One of my favorites, Siamese Rescue, is always looking for help transporting Siamese cats from shelters to foster homes or adoptive homes.[32] Some Siamese cats need to make their way from Florida or New York to Virginia or places west. Not wanting to trust these little beauties to an airline (for good reason[33]), Siamese Rescue started a little effort called the "Meezer Express" (Siameeezers). They recruited foster homes all over the country and now help forsaken, lost or surrendered Siamese and Siamese mixes all over America find new homes. (The older ones are called Meezer Geezers!) I have learned much and made lots of wonderful friends through my efforts to help Siamese cats through breed rescue, in memory of my sweet Sable, a lovely Siamese whom I adopted from a shelter in Germany and who lived for over twenty years. If you want to get involved with one of the canine breed rescue groups, just use the keyword on your Internet search engine for your special breed to find one that does rescue.

Some rescue groups, especially the ones that have no facility, are in need of volunteers to help get animals to the vet or the groomer, or from the shelter or pound to a foster home. There is a group in my town called the Animal Rescue Force that raised money to buy an R.V. Now they pick up the animals who are scheduled for euthanasia at the county pound and bring them to shopping centers around the county, where they try to adopt them out to good homes. (Prospective guardians must fill out an application and provide references, and a donation is required in order to adopt an animal.) The animals who are not adopted usually go home with a volunteer for a week for a second chance. If you have an extra bedroom or can accommodate another critter for a short time, consider offering your services as a foster parent for your local foster network. These are the organizations that may very well get behind your education efforts and sponsor your programs.

Or perhaps you are interested in offering your services to your local shelter as a neonatal caregiver for orphaned puppies and kittens. The jury is still out on whether it is a good idea to attempt to raise these little ones; some veterinarians feel that because they lack their parents they cannot become well socialized and will suffer from immune disorders. But if you believe in giving all living things a second chance and that the vets are not always right, you may want to call your local shelter and let them know you are willing to take in a puppy or kitten and feed him or her for about eight weeks until he or she is healthy enough to be put up for adoption. If you are really adventurous, get connected with a local wildlife rehabilitator and help out with injured or orphaned wild animals, too. There is not much controversy over their care, because they are not supposed to be socialized, anyway. Volunteering in these ways offers you experiences to share in your humane education programs as well as a valuable practical education for yourself.

If you like to speak out for animals, you may want to offer your services as a public speaker, humane educator or newsletter writer for your local rescue group. A lot of humane societies or rescue groups need people to help with website services. If you have some animal-related expertise—share! This could be as simple as visiting the PETA website, ordering a free video and asking teachers if you can show it during after-school programs or even during study periods.

The world is full of people who still believe that if you touch a baby bird you will get human cooties on it and the mom won't raise it. News flash: Birds cannot smell—not very well, at least. If you have a wildlife rehabber nearby and like to walk on the wild side, go volunteer to educate the public about wildlife issues, stay on top of pending wildlife legislation and help out in the clinic or driving the van once in a while. (Be sure that you are helping an actual sanctuary and not a roadside zoo or entertainment enterprise.)

Attend county commission meetings, open board meetings at your local animal regulation agency and municipal meetings, too. Be there as a voice for the animals. Or show up in court when you know there is an animal abuse case. Call your local television stations and let them know you will be there on behalf of the "victim"—the animal. Television cameras love opposing viewpoints. Judges and prosecutors will be much more likely to take animal abuse cases seriously if you are sitting in court taking notes so you can report back to national animal organizations. The victim can't be there, but you can. Take this opportunity to educate the public about why courts should take animal abuse seriously. Not only do we know it leads to future violence towards people, but someone who wantonly inflicts pain on an animal needs help. And he or she needs to understand that animal cruelty is a punishable offense.

Form alliances, too, with local youth groups and faith-based populations. Compassion is universal. Offer to show some videos and read some stories at churches, synagogues and other faith-based institutions. Invite a Catholic priest, minority minister or rabbi to hold a Blessing of the Animals at a nearby park in honor of St. Francis or Gandhi's birthday (the first week in October).

Need more ideas? This truly comprehensive and creative list was compiled and provided by Ann Gearhart of the Snyder Foundation for Animals:

Connections in Our Communities

- Before- and after-school programs: Providing humane education during these additional school hours is an excellent reinforcement or initial opportunity to get this information to the students.

- Veterinary practices: Humane education spay/neuter initiatives and our advocacy for consistent veterinary care for companion animals puts us alongside the veterinary community on these issues. Take a proactive approach and capitalize on opportunities to partner with veterinary practices in your community. Place public service announcements (PSAs)—your own, or those of national organizations—and a listing of your humane education programs at the veterinarian's office.

- Police department: The violence connection is a logical fit with police initiatives. Also, the Police Athletic Leagues (PAL centers) serve as both recreational and educational outreach within the community. Bite prevention programs such as those offered through State Farm Insurance are comfortable, instructive ways to participate in the safe community initiatives sponsored by police personnel.

- Department of Juvenile Justice (DJJ): The initiative to link character, humane and environmental education creates a new opportunity for us to work within the educational structure of DJJ. A variety of programs around the country, such as the Shiloh Project and Project Second Chance, are proof that such initiatives are worth the enormous time, effort and resources that it takes to get them up and running.

- Domestic violence coalitions: The connections between human violence and animal cruelty have been well documented. Presenting the American Humane Association (AHA)'s "The Link" initiatives to staff and personnel working with victims of domestic violence adds another dimension to humane education. Also, the Safe Homes/Safe Pets project can be a community partnership between animal shelters and women's shelters. Be familiar with all of the national organizations that are on the front line of providing both information and support to child protection and sexual assault services. Programs offered by these organizations include The Link (AHA), First Strike (HSUS), Breaking the Cycle of Violence (The Latham Foundation), and Family Vision (ASPCA). Being able to provide this helpful information can be an excellent bridge to fostering new relationships with vitally important organizations in our community.
- Museums: Within the collections of many museums can be found many representations of animals in art. Some museums have docents who have created tours specially designed around animal themes. If this is not the case in your community, volunteer to work with the museum to create such tours.
- Senior centers: Intergenerational programs have many social and community benefits. Try to initiate occasions when seniors and youth can get together and share animal-related reading material. The Animals ALOUD program, the Henry Bergh Book Awards, Operation Outreach materials and NAHEE materials are all excellent resources.
- Faith community: Celebrating the blessing of the animals

is just the tip of the iceberg for potential partnerships with churches, synagogues and mosques. "The Link" materials from AHA are good for teaching staff and adults. The human-animal bond can be traced back through scriptural history. Perhaps just posting PSAs on church bulletin boards could be the first step to fostering a new relationship in uncharted waters.

- Neighborhood community associations: These associations have historical significance in the development and continuity of neighborhoods across our nation. They not only meet in times of crisis, but also meet regularly to deal with issues regarding community safety. Humane education initiatives such as bite prevention, licensing, leash laws and feral cats are among the topics discussed at these meetings. By making yourself available to speak at these neighborhood meetings, you are also paving the way to become a part of many other institutions within the association.

- The media: Television, radio, and newspapers are the mainstream vehicle for communication. Everyone knows how important it is to foster positive working relationships with the people in these industries. Having your own weekly program may be too much to ask for, but a point person in the media who receives your PSAs is a vital link to humane education. A little-known radio service that exists in every state in our nation is the Radio Reading Network. This service provides daily programming for people with disabilities, primarily the visually impaired. Some subscribers to this service have guide dogs, but most do not. Making yourself available to provide information to this network would benefit individuals in your community who might otherwise not be reached.

- Red Cross: Emergency services for animals are now considered when educating our communities regarding disaster relief. Partner with your local Red Cross to become a part of their training and bring your expertise to enhance their service to the community.
- Service (gas) stations: In an attempt to educate people about the dangers of antifreeze, partner with area service stations to display posters and other informational materials.
- Parenting classes: "Child-proof your pet, pet-proof your child." Initiate opportunities to meet with parenting classes to provide information on how to meet (and protect) the needs of a companion animal when the new baby arrives, and the host of issues related to children and animals in the household.

These friendships and collaborations will be very valuable to you when you look for grant money, funding or financial aid. Grantors appreciate collaborations. There is power in numbers.

A final word about collaborations and grant opportunities: There are hundreds of books on the market (including Grant Writing for Dummies) for those who wish to apply for grants, so I will defer to those resources. If you decide to go for a grant, know that many school districts have specific grants for those who want to form partnerships with them. This information is usually available on their website or by calling their office of resource development. The purpose of these grants is to empower teachers who are interested in bringing unique programs to their classrooms. Others are available to anyone who is collaborating with a school project. A letter of determination from the Internal Revenue Service that grants an organization nonprofit status is usually a requirement to apply for most grants. However, if you are partnering with a school, sheriff's office or other agency that already has nonprofit status, you will not need your own.

Peter Bender of the Pegasus Foundation is in a position to approve grants, and his one pet peeve is grant writers who do not research the foundation first. "What is bad is when people call us and ask us simple questions that are answered on the website. It shows a lack of respect for our time and a lack of initiative on their part," says Peter. "The one important piece of advice that I can give is that those in search of grants fully research the foundation from which they are seeking money. Do the homework before making calls or sending proposals."

All that said, a humane education program does not have to cost you a bundle of money. There are lots of ways you can initiate a humane education program with little or no money. As mentioned in the list above, veterinarians make great partners in a humane education collaboration. They can't take time or staff away from their busy practices to get out and offer humane education lessons. However, they may sponsor yours, because having a presence in the community is so beneficial to their practice. If you are out teaching in classrooms, reading to dogs in libraries and showing up at street fairs wearing a T-shirt or polo shirt bearing the name of a vet or clinic, you are building goodwill in the community for that practice. Their name can be on coloring books or pencils or anything else you hand out while visiting schools and organizations. Insurance companies, too, have a stake in preventing dog bites and may sponsor a dog-bite prevention or animal communication lesson that you offer. And domestic violence agencies and organizations may help you spread the word about the link between animal cruelty and family violence by sponsoring workshops or programs that you organize and offer.

Think outside the box when it comes to finding ways to spread the word of compassion and kindness. You may find yourself giving or receiving help in unlikely places! Remember when Burger King announced their new BK Veggie, and People for the Ethical Treatment of Animals went so far as to advocate demonstrations in support of Burger King and posted a "Try the New BK Veggie" banner on their website? Always, always look for the common ground. Expand your reach with friendships, partnerships and collaborations. Your message is positive, optimistic and vital; helpful alliances are around every corner.

16

Outreach

Classroom teaching and organizing workshops are fine ways to reach your community with a strong humane education message, but there are even more ways to teach compassion through action.

Many of the large national organizations sponsor events throughout the year and ask grassroots activists to become involved on a local level. Here is a calendar of "animal days" that take place throughout the year.[34] Use it to help you plan events and activities, both large and small, throughout the year in your own community. With the sponsorship of local rescue and humane societies and animal-oriented businesses (such as groomers, pet sitters and pet supply stores) you should be able to get your event, and your message, off the ground.

January	
5	National Bird Day
13	Albert Schweitzer's birthday
22	National Answer Your Cat's Question Day
Varies	Chinese New Year (features a different animal every year)
February	is National Prevent a Litter Month
1	Serpent Day
2	Groundhog Day
17	Random Acts of Kindness Day
23	International Dog Biscuit Appreciation Day
27	National Polar Bear Day
Varies	Spay Day USA (an effort of the Doris Day Animal Foundation)
March	
1	National Pig Day
14	Save a Spider Day
21	First Day of Spring
20	Great American Meatout
April	is Animal Cruelty Prevention Month (ASPCA) and National Frog Month
3	Jane Goodall's birthday
7	Tag Day (American Humane Association [AHA])
10	ASPCA founded in 1866
22	Earth Day
23	Read Me Day (a day to celebrate children's books)
23	World Laboratory Animals Day
27	Arbor Day
27	Tell a Story Day
Varies	Easter
Varies	National Youth Service Day

May

1st week	Be Kind to Animals Week (AHA)
1	Save the Rhino Day
27	Rachel Carson's birthday
28	Sierra Club founded in 1882
Varies	Mothers' Day

June	is Adopt a Shelter Cat Month and Zoo and Aquarium Month
Varies	Fathers' Day

July

18	Cow Appreciation Day

August

3rd Saturday	National Homeless Animals Day (International Society for Animal Rights)
29	Henry Bergh's birthday (ASPCA founder)

September	is National Chicken Month
3rd week	Farm Animal Awareness Week
12	National Pet Memorial Day
22	Elephant Appreciation Day
23	Dogs in Politics Day

October	is Adopt a Shelter Dog Month
1	World Vegetarian Day
4	St. Francis Day
27	Make a Difference Day (Points of Light Foundation)
31	Halloween

November

1st full week	National Animal Shelter Appreciation Week (Humane Society of the United States)
2nd full week	National Children's Book Week

17	National Family Volunteer Day
Varies	Thanksgiving
Varies	Fur Free Friday (Friday after Thanksgiving)

December

10	Festival for the Souls of Dead Whales
21	First Day of Winter
25	Christmas
28	Endangered Species Act Signed in 1973
Varies	Chanukah

The *ASPCA Humane Education Resource Guide for Teachers*, which sells for under $10, not only lists these holidays but offers corresponding activities and lesson plans. For example, for the days that call for appreciation of cows, chickens and elephants, your lessons can be about those animals specifically. For non-animal days such as Earth Day and the first day of spring, lessons can be about the habitats that animals live in, how they prepare for changing seasons and how the human species has harmed the environment or is working to protect it. Lessons around Mother's Day can be about animal mothers and how they transport and protect their young (like opossums) or baby farmed animals such as veal calves and young hens.

But some of the other days call for much bigger recognition opportunities than simple classroom teaching. For example, March's Great American Meatout (sponsored by the Farm Animal Reform Movement) is a great opportunity to hold a veggie barbeque at a public park and invite anyone who would like to try the new veggie burgers, ribs and "chicken" products on the market. This food is readily donated by vegetarian food manufacturers and provides a wonderful opportunity to raise awareness of the health benefits of a plant-based diet. The tie-in with a major national organization has many benefits, since press releases, national news campaigns and media are all taken care of for you![35]

Spay Day USA offers an excellent opportunity to talk to local vets and clinics about reducing their rates on sterilizations for a week and promoting the health benefits of early sterilization, and Be Kind To Animals Week brings with it a component that has kids reading books about animal kindness.

One of my favorites of these annual campaigns is National Homeless Animals Day, a project of the International Society for Animal Rights (ISAR)[36] Although it is meant to raise awareness of the fact that millions of animals are euthanized every year in the United States, I have come to appreciate it more as a funeral or memorial service for the animals who have died in our local county facility. Some argue that the only people who come to these events are those already involved in animal advocacy and therefore we are always "preaching to the choir." But that does not matter when it is a funeral for your friends. Of course only those acquainted with the deceased come to his or her funeral, and so it is with the Homeless Animals Day Candlelight Vigil. Still, the media comes out and the message is brought home again: Spay and neuter your animals, keep them inside and on a leash, and yours won't be among the statistics of those killed every year. Thus the vigil is a form of humane education.

Here is an example of how to put on a National Homeless Animals Day event. It is always the third Saturday of August. I have provided this step-by-step procedure to demonstrate how simple it is to put on such an event. It is a lot of work, but it is not rocket science and it can easily be performed by one or two committed people.

- First, visit www.isaronline.org for a complete kit for organizing your vigil. In it, you will receive pre-written press releases and proclamations to send to your mayor and governor.

- Send the proclamation to the mayor or governor. This may take some time, so do it right away. Your mayor may ask you to attend a city hall meeting and read the proclamation into the record. This gives you access to all the city leaders, press and citizenry.

Gather a few friends—recruit them over the internet, via phone calls, over several glasses of nice Irish whiskey, whatever it takes! There is enthusiasm in numbers. You can ask some of the national organizations such as the HSUS or People for the Ethical Treatment of Animals (PETA) for their list of activists in your area. They will send you a list of all their members who have given permission to have their contact information given out.

- Find a location. I have used local shelters, local veterinary clinics, the county animal care facility, the beach or the back lawn of the town hall, library or county park. You may have to pay a small fee for using city property, or they may donate it.

- Plan your activity. You may wish to include a blessing of the animals and invite the local rabbi, priest and minister (or all three). I have found this an excellent way to reach out to the faith community, particularly minority churches, which may even bring along a choir and sing familiar hymns with animal-adapted lyrics. If you invite them, they will come. No minister will turn down a chance to preach to a captive audience about compassion towards animals. If you would like to assist them by providing animal-oriented scripture, they will be most accommodating.

- If an outdoor event at night is not your forte, think about planning a vegetarian luncheon to honor those who help animals. Keep in mind, however, that the event is a somber one. Remember that this is a national day of mourning and memorializing all the animals killed in the previous year.

- Visuals make great aides. You can use the paper collars commonly used in shelters to make a paper chain. (Unfortunately, in Palm Beach County, Florida, the chain has three thousand links to signify the number of animals killed each month.) Get some volunteers (students, perhaps?) to write names, excuses for surrender and ages on the collars to help drive the point home.

- Consider buying a banner (they can usually be purchased for under $100), and put it up wherever your event will be to attract the public. "Candlelight Vigil For Animals. Everyone Welcome" is one suggestion for the banner.

- Send an email, letter or flier to all the rescue groups and shelters in your area asking them to join with you in remembering the animals. You can get a list of these organizations from your local county animal control agency or your regional HSUS office. If they can't help you, try www.switchboard.com, and put in "animal rescue" under "Type of business." You will get a comprehensive list, including addresses and phone numbers.

In my community, six rescue groups, the sheriff's office, the mayor's office and the county facility have all joined together in the past to present the vigil. After the blessing and sermons, attendees are invited to walk their dogs in a procession along a populated street, along a waterfront or on a beach to make for an impressive photo opportunity for the media. Press releases should be sent out at least two weeks before with follow-up phone calls (see chapter fourteen). The two weeks gives news outlets time to put the event in their community calendars. Also, offer to write an article for the local paper to generate interest. You will find all the facts and backup information you need on ISAR's website.

I believe in this effort because the problem of overpopulation is a crisis that condemns millions of companion animals to death every year at an expenditure of millions of taxpayer dollars. Unwanted animals are brought into this world by irresponsible owners, and we need to educate our communities on the importance of spaying and neutering companion animals to stop the killing. Once again, education is at the forefront of helping our community to be better, stronger and more compassionate.

And remember, classroom teaching itself can constitute "outreach" in ways that aren't always obvious. Teaching students new ideas will give them something to bring home, thereby reaching out to more than just those students you see, but also their families and friends. Kids love to share new things with their parents, to come home from school and burst in the door shouting, "Mommy, know what?" They proudly share with their parents the new information that they have received, and this is the sprouting of the seeds we are planting.

17

Candlelight

"It is better to light one candle than to curse the darkness."

—Chinese proverb

"Professionally trained humane educators are a rare and precious breed," believes Lt. Sherry Schlueter. How right she is! There are currently about a hundred humane educators working professionally in the field—that is, people who are paid to teach humane education and are not expected to perform other shelter tasks or animal control duties at the same time. There are countless others who work in shelters or animal control facilities who are called upon to teach humane education from time to time, or give a shelter tour or set up a special event, but their main responsibilities are not those of a humane educator.

Consequently, humane educators have a relatively lonely life. Usually, if there is a humane educator on staff, he or she is the only one. There are rare occasions where there is more than one humane educator on board, but those situations are few and far between.

Ask humane educators what they feel is their most important job and the overwhelming response is "teaching empathy." In a survey of humane educators, empathy was the concept that humane educators felt was more important to teach than any other. If we can inspire empathy for non-human animals in the students whose lives we touch, who knows where that will lead? My favorite animal slogan has always been "It's not about loving animals, it's about respect." I have found that this speaks to the issue more than any other. We are not asking America's children to all turn into animal lovers, but we do hope that we can instill a sense of empathy and respect for all of earth's creatures, especially those who cannot speak for themselves.

"Empathy can be encouraged and demonstrated, and is a form of teaching," says Lt. Schlueter, "To be a role model is to be a teacher, and to exhibit qualities that others admire or aspire to is a form of teaching, and I think simply enlightening people about animal issues is a form of teaching that can cause behaviors to change. I have witnessed the transformation of lives due to the illuminating effects of information. This benefits all of us—animals, people, the planet. By example, you teach."

What about the negative messages that children may be getting at home from parents who have never learned empathy and therefore cannot model this behavior? Sherry believes that we can not only counter bad parenting but change minds if the information makes sense and is presented in a way that is palatable and understandable to the learner or listener. "It has to be taught in a way that allows a person who has done inhumane things, who has perhaps lived an existence of insensitivity, to save face and make changes. It all depends on how the message is delivered—the sincerity with which it is delivered and the quality of the person delivering the message. It is people who walk the walk and don't just talk the talk that get through to people. You can take a person who doesn't care for animals and give them a background in humane education and send them out there and they can, by rote, talk the talk, but they are not going to modify anyone's thinking. The energy and the sincerity and the passion of people who really take these issues to heart is what changes the world. And I do believe that we change the world one person at a time, so the quality of the person who is doing the teaching does matter greatly.

"I believe that the most important thing to teach others is that animals other than humans do think and reason, and are self-directing, and they can suffer in the same ways as the human animal can," continues Sherry. "I think it is a lack of understanding of the capacity to suffer that causes many people to be indifferent to other animals. It's that issue of "us" and "them"; it's the issue of the superior intellect vs. the inability to verbalize. There are people still walking around today who don't believe that animals can think for themselves, or reason things out, can make choices and can suffer emotionally, psychologically, intellectually. There are still people who don't acknowledge that animals can suffer physically. There are many who have been taught to be indifferent to animals and to view their own species as superior and everyone else as lesser beings with fewer capacities. I think that if we can teach the world that we are much more like animals than we think—every animal is an individual, just as every human is an individual—I think that if we could merely sensitize people to that, all of the rest of it could fall into place without the formal education. If you can't get that concept, then it is just us saying 'It is wrong to be mean to animals because it is immoral.' That's not gonna cut it. People have a responsibility in whatever capacity they come into contact with children or adults not only to look out for and protect others but to educate others and to encourage, as early on as possible, gentleness, kindness and compassion towards other living things. Without that, we are doomed to keep repeating the same mistakes and to live in a world where violence is the norm. Nobody can overlook the importance of teaching kindness and gentleness towards animals, because it will build character and understanding, which will lead to behaviors in life that will benefit human members as well as nonhuman members of society in our lifetime."

Well said, Sherry!

If you are considering making your mark in humane education either as a professional or volunteer, here's a chance to see what others in the field truly feel about their mission in life. Some of them face huge challenges with minimal resources; others are working in more nurturing and enlightened areas. The one thing that many of the humane educators surveyed agreed on is that they are not always reaching their stated goals of making the world a better place for both humans and animals by teaching compassion and empathy. Take the case of Jennifer Draggoty, Humane Educator for the New York ASPCA. "Reaching a huge population is very challenging," she said, "and we are competing with apathy from the schools, the public, home and parental influences that are at odds with our message, and, of course, negative messages on television." She finds she gets discouraged sometimes, too. "For a while there I was really angry and getting depressed and I did not want to take it out on the kids. But now I feel more balanced. I understand now where people are coming from. I can't blame the kids. When I first went in I was so excited; I was so sure I could change the world, change them. But that doesn't happen. In this position, you still hear about throwing cats or dog fighting—actually you're exposed to much more of it—and you get overwhelmed. But then it becomes clear that the best thing you can give them is education. You internalize what humane education is. You find a balance, you find your place. You settle in and find what works for you." Anyone who has seen *Animal Precinct* on Animal Planet can relate to the challenges Jennifer faces.

Jane Deming is a humane educator with the Providence Animal Rescue League in Rhode Island. She agrees that the job of a humane educator is not always easy. "You walk into a classroom and you never know what you will see or hear. So many teachers have let go of it all. It doesn't matter what foul language the kids use, or what their behavior is; the teachers are so stressed and can only deal with one thing at a time. That lack of respect for authority has really changed the environment that we are in. The other thing, I find the frustration comes in waves. It comes in highs and lows, peaks and valleys. I have an incredible interaction with a child, or an incredible revelation, and I go home and I am on top of the moon! Flying high! I know I did something really great—and then the next day I go into school and some kid will say "We found a big nest of snakes and we poured lighter fluid on it and lit them on fire." And then I feel, "Oh my God, I am not doing enough!"

"Sometimes it gets really frustrating because we know we are doing our best and we don't see it succeeding," says 2002 Humane Educator of the Year Ann Gearhart of the Snyder Foundation for Animals. "There is still dog fighting going on in the neighborhood, and people are still being inhumane to one another as well as to animals. Somehow you have to pull yourself up and not get angry or depressed, try to find the balance. I don't know that any of us find the balance. There is a part of me that is infuriated about going out and talking about spay/neuter with young children who have no control over whether their animals are going to be spayed and neutered because they don't take them to the clinics, they don't pay for it. So I am not doing the hard sell on that. My idea is to introduce the terminology and the concepts. Then, maybe, when they are old enough to make those choices and those decisions, that terminology won't be foreign to them. There will be something positive from that experience that they will be able to plug in to making that choice and that decision."

Janice Mininberg is with the Women's Humane Society in Bensalem, Pennsylvania and one of the co-authors of the *Humane Education Guidebook*. She remembers the moment she lost her balance and found it again. "I was at a meeting when we were working on the *Guidebook* and everyone had gone off to get lunch and it was just myself and Mary Ann.[37] I burst into tears. I told her that I needed to quit, I couldn't handle it anymore. I was getting so depressed. It felt beyond burnout; it was a complete meltdown. The people are still bringing animals in, the kids are still beating the crap out of the animals, the people still turn them in for all these ridiculous reasons and the thing that bothered me the most was whenever I would hear the kittens meow, the babies that came in. I knew we couldn't adopt them out, and I would run to the bathroom and start crying. I told Mary Ann about that, and the one thing that literally changed my life like day and night was something so profound that this teacher of teachers said to me. She said, "This is the one thing I tell all my students: You are in there to do one thing and one thing only; you are there to disseminate information. If they take that information and do something with that, wonderful! But you will never know. The only job you have is to disseminate that information in the best way you possibly can—that's it.' It took such a weight off my shoulders. All of a sudden I could breathe again!"

Lt. Schlueter remembers what caused her to go into the line of work that she has made a lifetime commitment to. "From my earliest memories I was interested in particularly protecting animals, like most of us who continue on into adulthood in professions or causes involving animals. For most of us this was a very early trait and we can't always explain it. There was no single event, there was no epiphany. It was there from my earliest memories, and I can recall being ridiculed for my extraordinarily empathic concern for animals. I have always considered it to be a deep and inescapable empathic nature that has been the reason for my work and my lifestyle.

"I remember my rescuing bugs and frogs and even saving plants with my sister Shelly. I have always felt compassion and empathy for both animals and humans, as evidenced by the complexity of the division I created, Special Victims and Family Crimes. I specifically wanted to include other vulnerable beings such as animals and children, the disabled, the elderly and anyone targeted because of disabilities or gender or lifestyles. I have never forgotten that people are animals too. I argue that when I speak to animal people who say "I hate people, I love animals." I always try to view human beings as upright primates, and that helps me sometimes to act more compassionately towards human beings. I also recognize that human beings are products not only of their genetic makeup but of their environment and their experiences and they are not always completely responsible for their actions. They are sometimes a product of what has happened to them as well. Just as I would act compassionately toward a dog that acted viciously because of his experiences with humans, so would I act compassionately toward a human being who did terrible things to others because of his past. I am not saying I would not want to hold human beings accountable, but I am not judgmental in that regard. I have dedicated my life to this work because it is what matters to me most. It's not just about animals; it's about complete intolerance for those who would oppress, exploit, abuse or target vulnerable others. I simply cannot tolerate or stand by and witness or allow those things to happen if I have the power to stop it.

"Most of the time I do not experience regret that I am not doing enough, and I think that the reason for that is that I do this twenty-four hours a day. By that I mean that even in my capacity in the law enforcement officer at this command level, running this dream section that I created, I am constantly bombarded with questions and the need for assistance. It is only due to my long experience at this and my expertise that I am very confident that I can respond accurately and appropriately to almost anything that anyone asks about or needs help with. This is a source of satisfaction—to know that you are the 'go to' person and that you have the answers and you can't really be stumped because you know it so well."

Sherry believes that anyone who wants to be a humane educator has to have a passion for animals first and foremost. "Humane educators can be formally trained individuals who have prior knowledge about these issues and who are knowledgeable about animals, at least sufficiently so to teach others the basics about care and to talk about the issues in society that affect animals most profoundly. But in reality, I believe that in a less formal way, all of us who care about animals, who work on their behalf, who empathize with their suffering and who have involvement with them, can be educators in a certain regard."

Kelley Filson of the San Francisco Society for the Prevention of Cruelty to Animals believes that her role as a humane educator is to get people thinking about what they have learned and determine if they are using it. And, she asserts, just like a doctor, police officer or lawyer, humane educators don't stop being humane educators when they leave work. There is no clock to "go off." "Humane education is a lifestyle. It is not a job," says Kelley. "Humane education does not end when you leave work, when you leave your classroom. I am always a humane educator, and it goes along with new avenues for humane education. When I am in a bar and everybody orders chicken wings, I talk about it. I tell them that they are eating something that was harvested from a six-week-old creature. I don't always change people's minds, but they listen.

"Human behavior is interesting and weird and sometimes screwed up. That other people can know all of the things that I know and yet choose something different is fascinating and infuriating to me. So I am always learning, too. I don't think it means they don't care, but being a humane educator is hard because it is a lifestyle. It's the little things that you can do. If you are a strict vegetarian and believe in the concept of animal rights but are employed by a shelter that only cares about cats and dogs, you have to separate your "work" humane educator from your "lifestyle" humane educator. So if you have a strong animal rights orientation, be sure to balance that. If they ask you to come in and discuss vegetarianism, ask them to invite a cattle rancher to come in, too. Then it becomes a life lesson. You are teaching life lessons about how to evaluate information; it's a lesson in critical thinking."

Two of the humane educators who were interviewed for *Canines in the Classroom* are incredible women working in extremely challenging arenas: Indian reservations. Linda Jo Fields-Horse is the lone humane educator working on the Winnebago Tribe reservation in Nebraska. Her goal is to teach the people on the reservation that there is so much more to our advocacy for animals than just "catch em and kill 'em." "We offered a workshop for the housing authority so that we could teach them what to look for with regard to illegal animal fighting. They are always on the grounds fixing things, looking out for the residents. I wanted to teach them what to look for. I am going to offer this workshop for the police department, too. We have a tribal council to pass laws, but this thinking about animals, this is all new to them. They consider themselves sovereign; they have their own rules and regulations. I want them to see animals are part of the reservation, part of the community."

Why does Linda take on this incredible challenge? "I belong to the wolf clan. The Wolf Clan takes care of the tribe; that is our role. Each tribe has its own clan system. There are the thunders and waters clans, healers and decision makers, the warriors. I feel like the animals are part of my tribe, too; I need to care for them. I love what I do. I grew up with a lot of animals. We were taught to be responsible, from my father and my grandfather. Growing up now, you don't see that at all. You see too much drinking, drugging, gambling, and kids left home alone. You can make yourself available through animal programs for them or you can just turn around and ignore it," says Linda.

But it isn't easy. Linda Jo Fields Horse faces the same kinds of animal cruelty seen in big cities all over America. "We deal with animal hoarding, dog bites, cruelty, abuse, everything all the big cities have, but nobody has ever dealt with it or is even aware of it. We are trying to do more spay/neuter education. We are pushing for a no-kill nation, but there are times we do euthanize; we have to. The teachers on 'the res' are very closed-minded. It is hard to get a foot in there. Right now I am getting little toes in there a few at a time. I offer classes at the wellness center such as dog-bite prevention, companion animal care and dog fighting. I am seeing the teachers' attitudes changing very slowly but I believe it will come."

Linda thinks that a big problem with the people on the reservation is the abject poverty in which they live. "We receive government funding, free food and health care. If we were to get help with veterinary care that would help a lot. We want to educate people to keep these animals in their homes." She stresses that education is the key to keeping animals at home. But she doesn't feel totally alone out there on the reservation in Nebraska. "I have the Humane Society of the United States (HSUS) regional office, the National Animal Control Association (NACA), and the American Humane Association (AHA); there are a lot of associations out there willing to help.

"Animals open the door and help us get in there and help with other areas of their life too. We give them something they can choose, something positive. We have two kids coming up now whom we worked with through our wellness center and who want to be vet techs, working with animals. Going through the program has really helped. . . . I believe that the children are buying into it because when they see me now their attitude is no longer 'Run, it's the dogcatcher lady, she's gonna kill my dog.' Now it's 'Hey, can you look at my dog? See what's wrong, my dog hurts.' You are there to help them and they understand that.

"This comes from being around them, in their classrooms, in the programs. Parents are not really behind it, but as long as the kids keep pushing for it the parents will come around. We have changed quite a few parents' minds that were real negative, real hard on us and wanted us to close down. Then they came down to see us, to see what we do, and now they are more supportive. We found some grants, a little help.

"I need to help people understand and stop mistreating these animals, whether it is a dog or cat, an iguana or a snake. They need to learn that an animal is not a novelty thing; it's a living thing to whom you make a commitment for life. Animals love you for who you are, and they want only love in return. It is heartbreaking when I see kids being cruel to animals. It hurts me; it's painful to watch. To watch them turn around, though, you get so much out of it. It's a lot of work to start with and it will always be a lot of work. It helps that it is coming from someone from their own community. I lived in a city for a while and I saw the attitudes of the people on the reservation. I am Native American but because I didn't live on the reservation they didn't hear me. 'You don't have to live here,' they would say. After I came back to the reservation I found a better response than when I was living outside the reservation. I was right in town, I was right there. I was one of them again. What makes me get up in the morning is the end of the day when at least one person says to you, "All right! You helped my dog!"

The other humane educator working with a Native American population is Nathania Gartman of Best Friends Animal Sanctuary. Poverty is certainly a problem on the reservation, she says, but so is the history of systematic, institutionalized abuse of the children. "Respect for life and the animals and respect for others is so important to the Navaho. Child abuse and animal abuse and domestic violence, which are all happening on the reservation right now, are not part of tradition. You find that nowhere in the early culture. Navaho children were taken from their parents and sent to live in boarding schools. It is part of this legacy of abuse from the boarding schools. The kids were beaten if they spoke their language or told their stories or referred to anything from their culture. They were literally beaten. So what you see now when we talk about the relationship between animal abuse and human violence on a cultural level is the legacy of abuse by the boarding schools, and most of those schools were government schools or mission schools. These kids were beaten by teachers, ministers, nuns, priests and administrators, and it was horrifying. It was a complete cultural disintegration. So people's response to how animals are treated is a direct result of the legacy of the boarding schools.

The schools and tribes and the communities as a whole are healing themselves and addressing domestic violence issues and addressing the cultural disintegration issues. The more the community does to heal itself, the better it is for the animals. So if you are working in a Native American community and care about animals, and you are not also working with the Boys and Girls Club or working with domestic violence issues, you are wasting your time. The tribes have to heal, they have to reclaim their true identity and reclaim who they are and then be able to be in tune with our relationship with a modern society that makes sense to them. The Navajo people used to live in these tiny communities with few families. They had the sheep and the goats and the animals are all around and everything was being taken care of in the same way. So if the animals are not being fed it was probably because the people weren't being fed, either. It was the nature of the community and everybody got treated in the same way. And when all of those native and cultural stories disintegrated it created a shift within the whole community.

"There is a new development on the Navaho reservation that is just beautiful. It is comprised of modern homes; it could be a development you would see anyplace. Every home has a fenced yard. You would not have seen that five years ago or ten years ago. So they are moving into communities and creating a different situation. In the whole tribe there are only a few animal control officers for the entire Navaho nation of 180,000 people. So you don't have the situation that you have in a city, where animal control comes in and picks up all the animals and, depending on the situation, euthanizes them. People now have animals in their homes and in their fenced yards just like in any other community. And you see change in the grocery stores on the reservation. When I started ten years ago there were no grocery stores on the reservation. If people needed to go shopping there were little trading posts where people could get milk or eggs or stuff like that, but they had to go to Flagstaff, two or three hours away, to go shopping.

Now there are grocery stores and they actually have a pet section that carries quality dog food, leashes, collars, beds, toys, all of it. So people are obviously buying it or the store wouldn't have it there. More people are living in communities and there is a movement to get more business to move to the reservation that is owned by Navaho.

"There is a veterinarian in Shiprock, the next one is in Tuba City, four hours away, or Farmington, over an hour again. There are vans that come in during the spring and summer months that offer spay/neuter. The Navajo nation has a puppy program and they work with Arizona Humane Society. There is a Second Chance program in Flagstaff that will be a shelter primarily to rescue dogs from the res. The Arizona Humane society will take up to sixty animals a month from that program and find homes for them in Flagstaff. There is a puppy program where families on the res can foster puppies and the Navaho nation will get them spayed and neutered and feed them until they are old enough and be adopted. There is a lot happening, but people off the res are not aware, and then they make these assumptions that nobody on the Navaho nation cares about their animals and it's not true. It's true of a lot of ethnic communities that we need to understand their stories and sort them out. Whether we agree with the stories or not, is irrelevant. These are the stories and we need to work with them. We have to start where they are and work with them."

These educators and others like them are lighting candles all over the country instead of cursing the darkness. Tracey Stevens-Martin is with Contra Costa Animal Services in Martinez, California. She believes that teaching children compassion for animals at a young age has a lifelong impact on every aspect of their future endeavors. She, too, faces multicultural challenges and a variety of languages and attitudes. But she is learning to pass on lessons learned from her own mother, who, she says, taught her how to overcome obstacles and that kindness always makes a difference, that love is missing everywhere and that we should never stop "sharing our love" of animals with the world. For those children who did not have a mother to teach them those lessons, humane educators fill an incredible need.

And what do seasoned humane educators have to say to you who may be just starting out?

Be brave. Be optimistic and do your best. A humane society is at stake.

Afterword

By Michael Berkenblit, DVM

Animals provide richness and texture to our lives; they reintroduce spontaneity and laughter in our over-structured and intensely planned days. As the twentieth century ends and the health-care community increasingly recognizes the damaging effects of loneliness and depression on human health, companion animals are taking on a new significance. By encouraging us to see the flowers, smell the night air and remember that we're part of a greater whole, they offer a source of emotional peace for people of all ages.

I have been reading for years about the research touting the benefits of raising children with companion animals. With children, animals contribute to the development of nurturance skills and self-concept. Increasingly, children are growing up without siblings, and many are adversely affected by divorce or parental illness. Companion animals enrich a child's life and buffer critical situations. In studies of families experiencing the death of a parent, for example, children with companion animals were better able to cope, and their ability to keep up in school was enhanced. Children raised with companion animals practice social behavior, develop tolerance, form friendships and learn sensitivity to the needs of another. For children with disabilities, an animal can provide critical companionship and serve as a "social lubricant" to encourage interactions with other children. In clinical studies, children raised with companion animals were less likely to be asthmatic.

I had engaged in all this reading in an abstract sense—I did not have any children to evaluate what happened when the 'rubber hit the road.' Four years ago, that all changed when I was truly blessed to become a daddy to Emma. Aside from being allowed to participate in the wondrous world of fatherhood, I also got a chance to observe for myself what the effects of companion animals were on children.

Since my wife and I are both veterinarians, we have had many opportunities to observe the relationship between the diminutive bipedal (Emma) and all the many quadrupeds in our home. I wasted no time in putting the two together. The day we brought our little bundle of joy home, I started photographing Emma and the family animals. One of my favorite pictures is of our seventy-pound Labrador retriever spread out on one end of the couch, with a small blanket at the other–which, when you look a little closer, contains a six-pound baby. The other picture, also from day one, is the peanut-like Emma, swaddled and snuggling with Katie, our Australian Shepherd. You can detect the look of resignation in Katie's eyes, as the concept of dropping down in the pecking order—from always being next to me in the chain of command, number two, as it were, to standing at number three—hits home.

I have always thought hard about the raising of puppies, and how it was both nature and nurture (genetics and environment) that determined the ultimate personality of the dog. Now I see with my own eyes how it is obviously going to determine our daughter's ultimate personality. As much as I would like to say that how we raise her will be important, I now see there is an inherent personality that I will have very little say in determining. One thing that I do know is that from a very early age, probably by two or three months old, when she was able to roll over and raise her neck, is that when we walked in her room in the morning when she woke up, she would glance up at our faces and then start looking at our legs, searching for all the animals.

Today, as a worldly-wise four-year-old, she feeds the dogs, lets them outside, puts leashes on them and gives them treats for sitting and coming on command. Now that Emma's hand at her side is the perfect height for Katie's prodding nose, she is often the inadvertent supplier of treats. Many times throughout the day I will hear a little voice complaining, "Hey! Katie!" as another bit of food is snatched from Emma's hand while she is not paying attention. She loves to put her princess outfits on our dogs, and when she is having a hard time falling asleep she requests one or two dogs in her bed to cuddle with. She loves to tell complete strangers about her dog Woody, who helps shy children read out loud, but says, "I don't call her Woody, I call her my 'Sweet Honey Dog.' " Emma has learned to be a sure handler of the animals—when Emma and I take the dogs to visit our neighbors, the dogs have a tendency to run in and check for full dog food bowls, and Emma goes in and toddles back out, holding two dogs by the collar

Emma is lucky to be raised in a house with two dogs that are Delta-Society certified for animal-assisted therapy. Other children are not so fortunate. The statistics for children being bittten by dogs are horrifying—one half of all children in the U.S. will have been bitten by the time they graduate high school! So for all the benefits that I see my daughter take pleasure in from being around companion animals—security, companionship, conversation initiators, and a test to her responsibility, I lament that other children have not been so fortunate.

It is my hope that once this book has been read and circulated, parents, teachers and anyone having to do with shaping children and therefore the world around us will see for themselves the miracle of kids and animals, and take to heart the words written on these pages. They are a blueprint for a compassionate, just and humane society.

Notes

1. In September 2003, Woody and Katie were honored for their therapy and education work when they were inducted into the Florida Animal Hall of Fame, a project of the Florida Animal Health Foundation, which seeks to educate people about the animal–human bond.
2. Stanley Coren, *The Pawprints of History* (Toronto: The Free Press, 2003).
3. Available from the Chicago Anti-Cruelty Society.
4. Available from Tribe of Heart at www.tribeofheart.org.
5. Available from www.veganoutreach.org.
6. Cited on the Web site "The Year of the Humane Child 2000: Facts on Kids, Animals and Violence," www.humanechild2000.0rg/index.html.
7. Ph.D. dissertation, American University, 2002.
8. First Edition, Washington, D.C.: National Congress of Parents and Teachers, [n.d.], p.3.
9. Mary Lou Randour, *Animal Grace* (New World Library, 2000), pp. 27-28.
10. Given by the Greater Del Mar Pa (Delaware, Maryland and Pennsylvania) Coalition of Humane Educators.
11. U.S. Department of Agriculture, Cooperative State Research,

Education and Extension Service.

12. The Delta Society, unlike Therapy Dogs International, the other major animal-assistance organization, welcomes animals of a variety of species—with the exception of snakes and spiders, for obvious reasons. This is why I chose the Delta Society over the other organizations. However, I am happy to work with volunteers who already have Therapy Dog International or Canine Good Citizen awards.
13. See www.SunshineonaLeash.org.
14. See PETA factsheet on exotic animals: http://www.peta.org/mc/facts/fsc4.html.
15. *Phi Delta Kappan*, December 2000.
16. For complete information on school projects involving aquarium fish, see www.DiveIntoFish.com.
17. From the Delta Society's *Standards of Practice in Animal-Assisted Activities and Therapy*.
18. Ibid.
19. From the Delta Society's *Team Training Course Manual*.
20. Cambridge: Harvard University Press, 2001. This is a fabulous "must read" for anyone interested in the bond between children and animals.
21. Marina Warner, *From the Beast to the Blonde: On Fairy Tales and Their Tellers* (New York: Farrar, Straus and Giroux, 1994).
22. From the CD *Teaching Peace* by Red Grammer (Smilin' Atcah Music, 1986).
23. *Teaching Compassion: A Guide for Humane Educators, Teachers and Parents,* The Latham Foundation.
24. Not his real name.
25. I later learned that Alvin and his mother had been arrested previously for the deaths of three pit bulls who had died from infections. The bodies were found on the property.
26. Jean Jacques Rousseau (1712-1778), French philosopher and author
27. David Hume (1711-1776), Scottish philosopher and writer
28. Clifton P. Flynn, "Exploring the Link Between Corporal Punishment and Children's Cruelty to Animals," *Journal of Marriage and the Family* 1999, Vol. 61: 975–6; also, Clifton P. Flynn, "Animal Abuse in Childhood and Later Support for

Interpersonal Violence in Families," *Society and Animals* 1999, Vol. 7, No. 2, 168.

29. *Family Relations*, 2000, Vol. 49, No. 1.
30. Unti, "The Quality of Mercy: Organized Animal Protection in the United States 1866-1930" (Ph.D. diss., American University, 2002).
31. Puppy mills are "puppy factories" where puppies are born of sick, weak and exhausted "brood bitches" who are killed when their usefulness is depleted. The animals are kept in squalor with very little care for the needs of the animals. For information about puppy mills go to www.helppuppies.com or www.nopuppymills.com.
32. For more information or to volunteer, go to www.SiameseRescue.org.
33. Cargo holds of airliners can be dangerous to animals because of the extremes in temperature, rough handling by flight crew and high numbers of lost animals every year.
34. Source: *ASPCA Humane Education Resource Guide for Teachers.*
35. See www.farmusa.org.
36. For more information, see www.isaronline.org.
37. Mary Ann Maggitti, Ph.D, West Chester University Early Childhood Education Dept. and co-author of the *Humane Education Guidebook.*

Appendix

Glossary of Humane Education Terms

Abandon. To leave an animal without care, food, water or shelter. To neglect the basic needs of an animal.

Alpha dog. The leader of a group of dogs; the strongest dog.

Animal. Any mammal other than a human being or any bird, amphibian, fish or reptile, wild or domestic, living or dead.*

Animal activist. A person who engages in activities that are designed to help animals.

Animal advocate. A person who cares deeply for animals and their well-being and who speaks out for them whenever and wherever possible.

Animal control. A government body that is charged with the responsibility of keeping the public safe from stray or dangerous animals and handling dog-bite cases, animal cruelty and other animal-related issues.

Animal control officers. County employees authorized to investigate crimes and issues involving animals. They are sometimes referred to as "ACOs."

Animal cruelty. The act of causing harm, injury or pain to an animal. Animal cruelty is a crime and a person charged with animal cruelty can be charged with a misdemeanor or a felony.

Animal-facilitated therapy. The use of animals to help people who are sick or dying.

Animal rights. A system of beliefs that revolves around animals having basic rights because they can feel, sense and experience pain and emotions. A person who believes in animal rights believes that animals are here for their own purposes and should not be used by humans for food, experiments, clothing or entertainment (i.e., rodeos, circuses, pony rides and petting zoos, horse-drawn carriages, etc.).

Animal rights activists. People who engage in organized efforts to raise awareness of animal causes that pertain to animal rights and are sometimes called "ARA's"

Animal welfare. The health and well-being of animals. Animal welfare advocates believe that the use of animals in entertainment, food and laboratories is acceptable as long as the animal is treated well. Humane societies are animal welfare organizations.

Baiting. The use of one animal to train another animal to fight. To use a small animal to make another animal angry and violent. Baiting is a crime.

Behaviorist. A person who is trained to help identify and solve common dog and cat behavior problems.

Bordetella. A virus which causes a cough and cold, also known as kennel cough.

Canine. Referring to an animal from the family canidae, which includes dogs, foxes, wolves and jackals.

Canine Companions for Independence. An organization that trains puppies to work with disabled people.

Carrier. A transporting device for small animals.

Cat condo. A large vertical cage which is used to house cats.

Catnip. An herb used to entertain and relax cats and kittens.

Contagious disease. An illness that can be passed from one person to another.

Citation. A written notice that a person may have committed a crime or infraction.

Collector. A person who has far too many animals for the housing available; sometimes called "hoarders".

Companion animal. A dog, cat, bird or other animal that is a part of the family and is a companion to the family members; a pet.

Confinement. The keeping of animals in an enclosed area from which the animal cannot escape. There are rules as to the proper confinement of an animal.

Crate. A cage used to house dogs.

Crating. The act of keeping a dog in a crate.

Cruelty-free. A designation that a product has not been tested on animals. (The product in question may or may not contain animal by-products.)

Euthanasia. The humane killing of animals by injecting them with a solution that brings on a coma and then death.

Exotics. Undomesticated (i.e., wild) animals such as chameleons, hedgehogs, iguanas, monkeys, sugar gliders and tigers, often shipped illegally to the United States and kept as companion animals.

Felony. A very serious crime, punishable by jail time or a large fine.

Fear biter. A dog who normally does not bite but may bite when he or she is afraid.

Feral. Wild and untamed. A feral cat is different from a stray cat in that feral cats have never been exposed to human beings, have never been tamed and are not friendly or able to be tamed.

First Strike. A national effort to encourage communities to become less tolerant of animal cruelty and more aware of the connection between animal cruelty and violence to people.

Flea. An insect that causes an infestation in dogs and cats, producing iron loss in the blood, severe itching and tapeworms.

Frontline. A product that prevents fleas and ticks when applied to the animal's neck.

Gentle Leader. A type of collar that is worn around the dog's snout and not his neck.

Guardian. The person responsible for the care of an animal, the animal's caregiver, the person who "owns" the animal.

Heartworm. A worm that infects the heart of a dog and is transmitted through the bite of a mosquito. Heartworms are preventable through the use of products such as Heartguard.

Humane. Pertaining to kindness, mercy or compassion.

Humane society. An organization dedicated to treating animals with kindness, helping animals in trouble and helping the community learn about animals and their care. Unlike animal control, humane societies do not make arrests, pursue investigations or take animals away from their caregivers.

Inbreeding. Causing animals with the same genes to breed, thereby possibly passing on defective genes.

Inhumane. Neglectful, abusive or cruel

Kennel. A place for boarding cats and dogs

Litter. Baby animals produced at one time by a single mother.

Misdemeanor. A criminal offense that is less serious than a felony.

Mistreat. To handle roughly or without regard to the animal's safety or welfare.

Mite. A small, microscopic parasite that lives off the blood of an animal. Ear mites are common in cats, and feather mites are common in birds.

Mutt. A dog that is the result of the coming together of dogs of differing breeds.

Muzzle. A device used to hold the jaws of a dog or cat tightly closed so that the animal cannot bite a handler or other animal.

Neuter. A word commonly used to describe an operation performed on a male animal, usually a dog or cat, that removes his ability to make a female animal pregnant.

Obedience training. Teaching dogs basic behaviors such as "sit," "stay," "lie down," and "leave it."

Overpopulation. Too many animals and not enough homes to place the animals. People who do not take responsibility for the animals they have and who do not spay or neuter them contribute to the overpopulation problem.

Pack. A group or family of wolves.

Parvovirus. A deadly disease in dogs that is very hard to cure.

Pet. A word used to describe companion animals.

Pocket pets. A term often used to describe small companion animals, such as guinea pigs, hamsters or gerbils.

Pride. A group or family of big cats such as lions.

Rabies. A deadly virus that is transmitted from one animal to another through the bite or scratch from an infected animal.

Rescue. Efforts to help animals who are stray or abandoned, injured or at risk.

Reptile. A cold-blooded animal such as a snake, lizard or toad.

Shelter. A place where stray or unwanted animals are housed until they are claimed by a guardian, adopted by a new guardian or euthanized.

Spay. To remove a female animal's ability to have puppies or kittens.

Stray. An animal that has lost his home or is abandoned.

Submissive behavior. Behavior that shows other dogs and people that the submissive dog is willing to follow and not be the alpha dog.

Tangled web theory. The theory first published by a psychologist and the F.B.I. that people who exhibit violence towards animals will be violent towards people.

Tapeworm. A long, flat worm that lives inside the stomach of an animal and deprives the animal of nutrition.

Tease. To annoy or pester. Teasing is frequently the cause of dog bites.

Tether. To tie an animal to a secure object.

Tick. A blood-sucking insect that attaches itself to dogs and cats that walk in high grasses or weeds.

Vegan. A style of living that avoids all animal and animal-based products such as meat, fur, leather and products that are tested on animals.

Veterinarian. A doctor who treats animals.

Veterinary technician. A person who assists a veterinarian with animal care.

Zoonosis. Zoonoses are diseases that can be passed between animals and people. The common cold, rabies and certain types of parasites are all examples of zoonotic diseases.

* Legal definitions such as this one, copied from a Florida

statute, are useful for pointing out that cruelty to snakes and turtles is "just as illegal" as cruelty to dogs and cats.

Woody and Katie's Book Recommendations

Children's Books

Agatha's Feather Bed, by Carmen Agra Deedy
Bertie Was a Watchdog, by Rick Walton
Cat Heaven, by Cynthia Rylant
Dog Heaven, by Cynthia Rylant
The Bookshop Dog, by Cynthia Rylant
Rats!, by Debbie Ducommun
Flute's Journey, by Lynne Cherry
Hey, Little Ant, by Phillip and Hannah Hoose
How Smudge Came, by Nan Gregory
If You Take a Mouse to School, by Laura Numeroff
If You Give a Pig a Pancake, by Laura Numeroff
(Oh, what the heck . . . anything by Laura Numeroff!)
Let's Get a Pup! Said Kate, by Bob Graham
Make Way for Ducklings, by Robert McCloskey
Night Rabbits, by Lee Posey
The Tenth Good Thing about Barney, by Judith Viorst
The Dancing Deer and the Foolish Hunter, by Elisa Kleven
Where Once There Was a Wood, by Denise Fleming

Adult Books

Animal Grace, by Mary Lou Randour
Companion Animals and Us, by Anthony L. Podberscek, Elizabeth S. Paul and James A. Serpell
Cruelty to Animals and Interpersonal Violence, by Randall

Lockwood
and Frank R. Ascione
Why the Wild Things Are: Animals in the Lives of Children, by Gail Melson
Good Owners, Great Cats, By Brian Kilcommons and Sarah Wilson
Good Owners, Great Dogs, by Brian Kilcommons and Sarah Wilson
Strolling with Our Kin, by Marc Bekoff

Spirit's Reading Recommendations

Books about Cats and Dogs

Whistle for Willy, by Ezra Jack Keats
I Want a Dog, by Dayal Kaur Khalsa
A Home for Nathan, by Claudia M. Roll
Sam, Bangs and Moonshine, by Evaline Ness
Can I Keep Him?, by Steven Kellogg
Search and Rescue Dogs, by Elizabeth Ring
My Buddy, by Audrey Osofsky
Orient, by Tom McMahon

Books about Other Animals

Animal Alphabet, by Bert Kitchen
Amos and Boris, by William Steig
Noah's Ark, by Peter Spier
Cactus Hotel, by Brenda Guiberson
Dream Wolf, by Paul Goble
Wolves, by Seymour Simon
The Big Snow, by Berta and Elmer Hader
Stellaluna, by Janell Cannon

Books about Birds

Make Way for Ducklings, by Robert McCloskey

Owl Moon, by Jane Yolen

Books about Trees

A Tree Is Nice, by Janice May Udry

The Lorax, by Dr. Seuss

And, if you like to draw animals . . .

Ed Emberley's Drawing Book of Animals

Ed Emberley's Drawing Book: Make a World

A Word about Spirit

BY ANN GEARHART

From No Name to a SpiritSong . . .

THEY SELDOM ARRIVE with a history or story—the homeless creatures with no names—disoriented, fearful, and alone. When it is their good fortune to find safety at an animal shelter, such as Baltimore County Animal Control, some of the story begins to change. First of all, they are now safe—safe from highways and difficult weather; safe from hunger and thirst; safe from the danger of careless or cruel people. Now, they have found a momentary respite.

Such was the case of a lanky, thin and skeptical hound dog, who found her way to the shelter via a brief stopover at a police station. Dragging a twenty-five-foot chain behind her, attached to a collar revealing nothing but its color, she arrived. Caring people looked after her, hopeful that the phone would ring with her description as a lost dog. It never did. An inquiry was received, however, from a person who knew that the best place to find a wonderful canine companion is from an excellent shelter—a turning point in the life of a No Name.

When do we need to bring an animal into our family? The answers to this question are numerous, but in this case the reason was illness. An exceptional education assistance dog, Sneakers, had been diagnosed with cancer. How long could she continue her work? Perhaps she needed to share all of her talents, skills, devotion to duty and love of life with a future assistance dog, while she was in treatment and still yearning to work. And so the search for a canine trainee began—phone calls, inquiries, questions and mystery—who would it be? And where would I find such a dog?

The answer in this case was Baltimore County Animal Control—a caring staff with the desire to provide good homes for as many animals as possible. A few more phone calls and visits and, for one lanky hound, life changed. The adoption accomplished, we took a quick trip to our veterinarian, who pronounced her in good health, then took a moment to whisper in one ear, "You'd better be a very smart dog" (knowing the expectations of her future work). In the other ear, she whispered, "This is the luckiest day of your life."

To complement her personality and the dogs who preceded her, we named her SpiritSong. From No Name to SpiritSong—the journey is just beginning. She is registered in an assistance dog program at Dog Ears and Paws, Inc., and after her training she will work as an education assistance dog for the Snyder Foundation for Animals.

On September 20, 2002 the United States Postal Service

and the American Partnership for Pets announced the Stamp Out initiative. Two spay/neuter stamps, one reflecting a cat and the other a dog, are bringing national awareness to the issue of pet overpopulation. We hope you are using the spay/neuter stamps for your everyday correspondence, and that each time you mail a letter you will think of the animals who have been adopted and have gone from a No Name to a SpiritSong.

Contact Spirit at The Snyder Foundation for Animals (410-366-0787).

Resources

The American Humane Association (AHA), founded in 1877, offers training workshops for volunteers, shelter workers, educators, social workers and more on the link between animal cruelty and violence to people. They sponsor special events and contests throughout the year to get kids involved in helping animals. They can be found online at www.americanhumane.org and have a "Just for Kids" site that offers fun facts and book lists.

The American Society for the Prevention of Cruelty to Animals (ASPCA) can be found online at www.aspca.org and has a tremendous amount of resources available for purchase online. I have found that a simple little book that sells for less than $10 is a most useful and critical tool. *The ASPCA Humane Education Resource Guide for Teachers* is packed with information about special monthly features, lesson plans, games and cyber hunts. The ASPCA also has a wonderful book list and a plethora of educational videos, posters, books and booklets in both English and Spanish. I also recommend *The Humane Education Guidebook*, a cooperative project of the Federated Humane Societies of Pennsylvania Education Committee and the ASPCA. This is a spiral notebook filled with ideas, lesson plans and even some theory as to how people learn. It offers tips and ideas on how to get started and how to build a presence in the community. The book sells for around $70 through the Web site of the Association of Professional Humane Educators (aphe.vview.org; see below), but Guidebook Workshop attendees receive the book as part of their workshop fee.

The Association of Professional Humane Educators (APHE) is one of a very few professional organizations dedicated to enriching the lives and activities of humane educators. They are a support system for humane educators and teachers in that they are raising the status of professional and non-professional humane educators and the standard of professionalism and uniformity among them. They offer seminars and workshops throughout the year that are well worth checking out. See www.aphe.humanelink.org.

The Humane Society of the United States (HSUS) has an educational component called the National Association of Humane and Environmental Education (NAHEE). NAHEE publishes *KIND News*, an award-winning classroom newspaper available in Primary, Junior and Senior editions. The subscriptions are sponsored by area businesses or humane societies and include lesson plans for teachers. NAHEE also offers professional development workshops called "Teach Kids to Care," which travel around the country training interested volunteers, teachers and others about setting up and facilitating humane education programs. The HSUS and NAHEE also have an area on their site where educators can visit to learn about books that have been recommended or that have won awards for their humane themes. I find this listing a tremendous help when searching for new books to include in my curriculum. See www.nahee.org.

The International Institute for Humane Education (http://www.iihed.org/) is one of the more professional organizations offering support and training for humane educators. There is even a degree program for those wishing to earn an advanced degree in humane education. Their Sowing Seeds workshops are enormously popular and take place throughout the year all over the country. They have an abundance of books, essays and literature available to humane educators and students. Their approach to humane education is holistic and all encompassing and they are a very well established and well-respected organization.

The Latham Foundation for the Promotion of Humane Education was founded in 1918 and has a rich tradition of promoting humane education through publications, funding, videos and books. They publish an excellent magazine, *The Latham Letter*, that is especially helpful to teachers, humane societies and educators with its timely news articles, topics and book reviews. The Latham Foundation sponsors seminars, produces videos and publishes books on the link between animal abuse and violence to people. See www.Latham.org.

People for the Ethical Treatment of Animals (PETA) has a humane education division that makes books, videos and pamphlets available to teachers and students on a wide variety of subjects. PETA's sponsored *Share the World* video is one of the most comprehensive and entertaining videos that I have seen yet, and the teachers I have given this video to rave about it. *Share the World* is comprised of four segments dealing with

a variety of animal issues. After each segment is shown there is built-in discussion time with suggested topics for conversation. *Share the World* is free for the asking and is a wonderful start for anyone's program and a vital part of any humane education program.
See: http://www.sharetheworld.com/index.html.

There are, of course, many other organizations and associations, but throughout my career as a professional humane educator, I have relied heavily on the above organizations to support my work. Help is there for the asking from all of these organizations. Some of the major organizations and shelters, such as Broward County Humane Society, The Pet Care Trust, The Chicago Anti-Cruelty Society, Best Friends Animal Sanctuary, Dumb Friends League and the Snyder Foundation for Animals have their own humane education programs and I have found that they are more than willing to mentor new educators. It would be beneficial to check with the largest shelter nearest you to see what programs they have available. Many of these organizations share their lessons and ideas or even have original materials to sell. I recommend the following resources in addition to those listed above:

Active Learning Corporation
P.O. Box 254
New Paltz, NY 12561
(845) 255-0944
www.activelearningcorp.com

The Delta Society
580 Naches Avenue SW, Suite 101
Renton, WA 98055-2297
(425) 226-7357
www.deltasociety.org
info@deltasociety.org

Doris Day Animal Foundation
227 Massachusetts Ave. NE, Ste. 100
Washington, DC 20002
(202) 546-1761
www.ddaf.org

Humane Education Advocates Reaching Teachers
(HEART)
P.O. Box 23
New Rochelle, NY 10804-0023
(212) 804-5714
www.nyheart.org
info@nyheart.org

National Parent-Teacher Association (PTA)
330 N. Wabash Avenue, Suite 2100
Chicago, IL 60611
(312) 670-6782
(800) 307-4PTA (4782)
www.pta.org

Psychologists for the Ethical Treatment of Animals
(PSYETA)
www.pyseta.org
info@psyeta.org

Vegan Outreach
211 Indian Drive
Pittsburgh, PA 15238
www.veganoutreach.org